Beyond Demographic Dividends

Series on Chinese Economics Research
(ISSN: 2251-1644)

Series Editors: Yang Mu *(Lee Kuan Yew School of Public Policies, NUS)*
Fan Gang *(Peking University, China)*

Series on Chinese Economics Research – Vol. 5

Beyond Demographic Dividends

Cai Fang

Chinese Academy of Social Sciences, China

社会科学文献出版社
SOCIAL SCIENCES ACADEMIC PRESS (CHINA)

World Scientific

Published by

World Scientific Publishing Co. Pte. Ltd.

5 Toh Tuck Link, Singapore 596224

USA office: 27 Warren Street, Suite 401-402, Hackensack, NJ 07601

UK office: 57 Shelton Street, Covent Garden, London WC2H 9HE

Library of Congress Cataloging-in-Publication Data
Cai, Fang.
   [Chao yue ren kou hong li. English]
   Beyond demographic dividends / Cai Fang.
     pages cm. -- (Series on Chinese economics research, ISSN 2251-1644 ; vol. 5)
   "Originally published in Chinese by Social Sciences Academic Press (China)."
   Includes bibliographical references and index.
   ISBN 978-9814520874 (alk. paper)
   1. China--Economic conditions--2000– 2. Labor supply--China. 3. Economic development--
China. I. Title.
   HC427.95.C33713 2014
   330.951--dc23

                2013038485

British Library Cataloguing-in-Publication Data
A catalogue record for this book is available from the British Library.

The Chinese Fund for the Humanities and Social Sciences provided funding for the translation of this book.

《超越人口红利》

Originally published in Chinese by Social Sciences Academic Press (China)
Copyright @ Social Sciences Academic Press (China) 2011.

In-house Editor: Dong Lixi

Typeset by Stallion Press
Email: enquiries@stallionpress.com

Printed in Singapore

Preface

As we usher in the 21st century, certain phenomena with regard to China's economy after the reform and opening up are difficult to understand. At first, peasant worker shortages spread from coastal areas to the entire country, and then wages of average workers continually increased over the years. Many people are under the impression that China has the permanent characteristics of large population and abundant labor supply. Therefore, it is hard to believe there are labor shortages in China, a phenomenon that has existed since 2004 and become more visible with corresponding wage increases.

The unexpected labor shortage actually follows the description of an economic growth period in development economics literatures, i.e., the growth rate of labor demand exceeds the growth rate of labor supply. Therefore, a turning point in the economic growth is imminent. As the description above is based on a dual economy development model, which is characterized with unlimited labor supply, and the theoretical model is associated with the name of Professor William Arthur Lewis, we call this turning point the "Lewis turning point."

As a scholar in development economics and an observer at the frontier of China's economic growth, I found that the Lewis turning point in China's economic growth had been approaching. The finding was widely questioned. However, until recently, those who long opposed the finding have not provided adequate empirical evidence to deny the arrival of the Lewis turning point. Despite this circumstance, I continued empirical researches to prove the finding from various angles, i.e., this is a phasic change. One part of my work is on the demographic factors that are related to the Lewis turning point.

Demographic transition comes with economic growth and social development. One result is the proportion of working-age population will rapidly increase, providing demographic dividends to the economic growth through sufficient labor supply and high savings rates. When dependency ratio is used as the index of demographic dividends, it has been found to decline at a decreasing rate for a long period of time and is predicted to reach the bottom in 2013 and start increasing afterward. In other words, demographic dividends are going to disappear. This finding is consistent with the finding concerning the Lewis turning point. It is not surprising that this finding was also questioned.

Time is working in my favor, and the changing reality is eliminating people's doubts on this phasic change. However, debates are continuing, with the focus on the following aspects: (1) the evidence of the finding; (2) the meaning of the finding; (3) the government policy implications of the arrival of the Lewis turning point. I continue empirical researches and publish papers in academic journals to respond to all questions and queries, and I also write short articles requested by newspapers and magazines to discuss the topic above in a less pedantic style. This book collects a series of representative articles.

Following editors' suggestions, this series of articles is arranged into six chapters, which discuss the same topic from six different angles. Chapter 1 is "The Arrival of the Lewis Turning Point," Chapter 2 is "The Disappearance of Demographic Dividends," Chapter 3 is "End of the Unlimited Labor Supply Era in China," Chapter 4 is "Employment Challenges After Reaching the Lewis Turning Point," Chapter 5 is "Further Propelling Urbanization and Balanced Regional Development," and Chapter 6 is "Avoiding the Middle-Income Trap." To extend the reading, each of the six chapters attaches an academic paper to provide the reader with more literatures and empirical evidences. This arrangement helps to overcome the unsystematic drawback of the collection of articles.

The world economic history shows that past success in a country's economic growth is not necessarily a promise of its success in the future. Especially when the country becomes a middle-income country, previous practices may not work well in future stages. Because of the arrival of the Lewis turning point and the disappearance of demographic dividends,

China will face many severe challenges and be in danger of falling into the middle-income trap during its 12th five-year plan or later period. Successfully dealing with these challenges helps to overcome this potential "trap" and realize the great goal of constructing a generally affluent society. I sincerely hope this series of work can help the readers to deeper thinking in relevant topics.

Contents

Chapter 1

The Arrival of the Lewis
Turning Point

1.1. How Many Turning Points will China's Economy Experience?

In daily economic life, "turning point" or "inflection point" is a frequently discussed topic: people talk about the "turning point" when the housing market or stock market experiences directional changes and about the "turning point," when there is shortage of peasant workers. In the economic road to modernization and affluent livelihood of its people, how many turning points will China experience? What is the meaning of each turning point? In fact, there are only three turning points with significant meanings in economic growth, and the passing of all of them will realize China's economic modernization and the wealthy lives of the Chinese people. Before introducing these three turning points, there is a description of a typical dual economy development model.

William Arthur Lewis, the 1979 recipient of the Nobel Prize in Economics, observed that a developing country's economy could be divided into two sectors: a traditional agricultural sector and a modern industrial sector. In the traditional agricultural sector, there is abundant surplus labor compared to land and other production input factors, resulting in much lower labor productivity compared to the modern industrial sector. At the same time, the modern industrial sector can extract the surplus labor from the traditional agricultural sector with fixed low wages during its growth and expansion. Labor supply is unlimited in the modern industrial sector, therefore, the rapidity of its growth and expansion fully depends on its ability to accumulate capital. This is the well-known process of dual economy development.

Note that wages can hardly increase until the characteristic of unlimited labor supply disappears. In addition, capital accumulation becomes the only bottleneck of economic growth, and governments aiming at accelerating economic growth usually use all possible methods to help accumulate capital. As a result, there will be a bias in their economic and social policies to protect investors instead of workers. In other words, reduction in income differentials can hardly be seen in the whole process of the two-sector economic growth. Simon Smith Kuznets, the 1971 recipient of the Nobel Prize in Economics, described this phenomenon: "with economic growth and increase of per capita income, income inequality is not reduced, but increases over a period of time."

Fortunately, one important characteristic in the process of the two-sector economic growth is that the traditional agricultural sector shrinks and the modern industrial sector expands gradually, with an important factor that labor continually transfers from the primary sector to the secondary sector to promote this process. It is exactly this labor transfer that leads to the three consecutive turning points.

The first turning point. The higher the growth rate of the modern industrial sector, the faster it attracts labor transfer. Meanwhile, the rural population grows at a decreasing rate, which is reflected in a lower growth rate of the working-age population. As a result, the growth rate of labor demand will eventually exceed the growth rate of labor supply. Then, facing abundant, but less surplus labor, the modern industrial sector must increase wages if the growth rate of rural labor demand remains the same. According to Lewis's definition, this is the "first Lewis turning point." It turns out that labor supply is no longer unlimited after reaching this turning point, though it is not an absolute labor shortage. It is more important that firms begin competing for labor and the wages of average workers increase.

The second turning point. Kuznets did not imply a continual increase in income differentials, but described the relationship of economic growth and income inequality with an inverted U-shaped curve. With economic growth, income differentials first increase to its maximum, and then turn to decrease. Therefore, Kuznet's turning point is a turning point of income distribution improvement. After reaching this turning point, income gaps decrease. Though the time at which this turning point is reached varies in different countries, it is related to the first Lewis turning point; the disappearance of unlimited labor supply leads to increases of average workers' wages and incomes, which help to reduce income differentials. Theoretically, the two turning points coincide, but in reality, whether the two turning points coincide depends on government policies. If government policies follow the changes in the economic growth, i.e., on one hand, enhance protection of workers' primary rights with necessary regulation, and on the other hand, maintain market selection and apply a more efficient incentive mechanism for labor transfer, then the two turning points should consistently coincide in theory and in reality.

The third turning point. This is an inevitable long-term result of the first two turning points. After reaching the first Lewis turning point, we know that there will be a labor shortage if wage is not raised. An increase in average workers' wages and directional changes of government policies will result in reaching the Kuznets turning point, which implies reduced income gaps. With better incentive mechanism and methods, labor will still transfer from the low-productivity, traditional agricultural sector to the high-productivity, modern industrial sector until labor productivities in both sectors are the same. Then, we will face the second Lewis turning point — sometimes, it is also called the commercial point, which indicates the disappearance of the dual-sector economic structure and the completion of the dual economy development process.

It was once said that we only need three thumb rules to understand the economic phenomenon. The three turning points mentioned above are such analyzing tools. In this framework, we will learn that the recently observed shortage of peasant workers is not an irrelevant phenomenon in economic growth; we will learn the significance of enacting the Labor Contract Law of the People's Republic of China; and we will also learn that accelerating a series of reforms, including the household registration system reform, is important to extending the labor migration from rural areas to cities and to ultimately lead China's transformation into an integrated, modernized economy.

1.2. Finding the Arrival of the Lewis Turning Point and its Policy Implication˙

The finding on the arrival of the Lewis turning point was hyped by news in 2007, but I actually raised the finding at an earlier time. Though most of my colleagues opposed it, I continued researches on this topic without participating in any arguments, because those who opposed this theory generally did not do any empirical analysis, but only raised opinions. Without serious empirical analysis, there is no ground to build any valid debate or argument. Both Australian National University and the Asian Development Bank held symposiums on the theme of the Lewis turning point, respectively, organizing people to criticize this finding. However, it also proves that the finding is critical for the analysis of both Chinese and Asian economies.

According to the definition by Arthur Lewis, the arrival of the Lewis turning point does not imply an absolute labor shortage, but a labor shortage with constant wages. Based on this definition and our current observations, I suggest not doubting this finding in policy analysis. However, it is free to argue for academic purposes since the nature of academic research is to seek common ground and reserve difference.

There is a policy implication for the arrival of the Lewis turning point. When finding that the Lewis turning point is imminent, I did not intend to underestimate the importance of employment, but instead, focused on raising three questions that we should pay attention to: (1) wage will rise at an increasing rate; (2) labor relations will experience acute change; and (3) it is extremely urgent to change the development pattern. No matter which finding is right, the problem becomes more obvious now, calling for attention to relevant phenomenon from policy makers and making use of economic and social development laws to solve the problem. I understand that policy makers who disagree that the Lewis turning point arrived are concerned that people will, in reality, overlook employment pressure. However, more evidences have shown that admitting the imminent Lewis turning point helps sharpen our thinking, preventing anyone from arriving at a trivial conclusion on employment.

The arrival of the Lewis turning point and its policy implication

The arrival of the Lewis turning point is the inevitable result of demographic structure changes. From the long-term labor supply and demand relationship, the increment of China's working-age population is decreasing over the years, at an annual rate of 13.6% from 2004 to 2011. This new trend, where the growth rate of labor demand exceeds the growth rate of labor supply, can be described with the concept of the Lewis turning point.

The arrival of the Lewis turning point is not a bad thing, but indicates the disappearance of the dual-sector economic structure (though it will take a long time for the disappearance of the dual-sector economy structure after reaching the turning point). It is shown as: (1) continual peasant worker shortages determined by the long-term demographic structure, which cannot be simply explained by cyclical and partial factors; (2) the increase of average workers' wages, which is a continuation of the wage increase trend since 2004 and is directly related to the new labor supply and demand relationship, the new generation peasant workers' expectations, and the improvement of rural family lives; and (3) new change in labor relations, which is reflected as the aggravation of conflicts between workers and firms.

The British magazine *The Economist* reported this argument recently, which was based on my previous paper and foreign scholars' retelling. The report suspected that it is too early for China to reach the turning point. Lewis did predict several possibilities for an early arrival of the turning point, but I do not think this is the case in China. So far, the wage increase has not exceeded the increment of the marginal product of labor.

First, average workers' wage increase and the improvement of labor productivity are synchronous in the past 10 years. Premier Wen Jiabao emphasized on this principle, and it should also be strictly followed in the future. In fact, Japan's national income doubling plan, made decades ago, also emphasized the support from the increase of labor productivity.

Second, since the wage increase was lower than the increment in the marginal product of labor in an earlier period, there will be space for a more rapid wage increase in this period with peasant worker shortages.

It is a good time to adjust income distribution, improve the primary income distribution, and increase the "two proportions" (the proportion of residents' income in the national income distribution and the proportion of workers' remuneration in the primary income distribution). China should not miss this opportunity because of unnecessary fears of the arrival of the turning point.

The groups facing employment difficulties in the labor market

The arrival of the Lewis turning point does not imply that employment difficulties will spontaneously disappear. China should pay great attention to employment not for the reason that labor supply exceeds labor demand. In contrast, more specific policies can be made if China turns its attention from the relationship of aggregate labor supply and aggregate labor demand to the main groups with employment difficulties in the labor market. During the financial crisis, the State Council and local governments paid great attention to the employment difficulties of peasant workers, college graduates, and unemployed urban residents. Since the three groups are related to three types of employment difficulties or unemployment (cyclical, structural, and frictional unemployment), the main problem in the new pattern of labor market can be targeted if the three groups' employment problems are solved.

There are two major changes in the employment of peasant workers. One is that agriculture is no longer the reservoir of surplus labor. Mechanized production and socialized management greatly reduced labor demand in the agriculture sector. From 2002 to 2008, labor per mu for rice, wheat, and corn production was reduced by about one third. The other is the generation replacement of peasant workers, that over 60% of peasant workers were born after 1980. The new generation of peasant workers cannot and does not intend to farm, which leads to irreversible labor transfer.

The employment difficulties that peasant workers face are cyclical unemployment shocks, which are reflected in the earlier home return during spring festival in 2009 and the shortage of peasant workers after spring festival in 2010. It is very important and urgent to provide them with more stable employment and the same labor protection (such as social security and employment assistance) as urban residents. Urbanization of peasant workers and their families brought by the household registration system reform can comprehensively improve employment in the labor market.

The employment difficulty that college graduates face is structural unemployment, which is caused by mismatches between their skills and the labor market demand and gaps between their job expectations and the real job vacancies. Appropriate adjustment of education structure, reform in higher education, job training, and other employment assistance services are the key to solving the problem.

Unemployed urban residents are characterized as older residents lacking in renewed skills. They are usually reemployed in unskilled job positions after their layoff. Since this group faces natural unemployment, which is the structural and frictional difficulties, the most important assistance to this group is to provide job training, profession introduction, and other services as well as increase social security coverage.

Trend in changes of labor relations

The experiences of western countries and developed Asian economies show that an obvious sign of the imminent Lewis turning point is the rapid changes in labor relations. With the new labor relations, workers are more conscious of guarding their rights for increasing wages and benefits and improving working conditions, while firms lack willingness to improve, which will result in an inevitable partial conflict between workers and firms.

Therefore, the current conflicts between workers and firms in China, such as strikes, are regular and inevitable. They should be considered the "growing pains," which cannot be, and are impossible to, avoid. More generally speaking, in the transition from a middle-income country to a high-income country, China faces as many challenges as it faced during the upgrade from a low-income country to a middle-income country. When the labor relations change in a society, conflict between workers and firms will usually be triggered or revealed. Meanwhile, people raise expectations of income increases, while a group of them will face difficulties in the adjustment. For example, during the U.S. manufacturing industries' transferring process abroad, many domestic workers were laid off and were unable to find new jobs. With every cyclical economic fluctuation that causes large manufacturing industry migration, employment is usually not recovered — so-called "jobless recovery." China is suggested not to set up labor market institutions to solve the problem and to prevent the conflicts. I think it is wrong to ignore or suppress the conflicts between workers and firms, since it is an "ostrich strategy."

Western countries, Japan, and South Korea have become high-income countries, while many Latin American countries are still in the middle-income trap. One important reason is how they learn from the "growing pains." Failures in Latin American countries were due to their populism policies, which made inflated promises and greatly raised the people's expectations. In the meantime, these countries neither dared to hurt vested interests nor kept their promises, which resulted in increased income differentials. Therefore, they had to turn to coercion policies that led to social unrest. In contrast, those developed countries painfully set up a complete labor market institutional framework that solved the conflicts and oppositions between workers and firms when friction between workers and firms was aggravated. There was no other choice for them, though this one was costly. Regulating and coordinating the relationship between workers and firms within the labor market institutional framework is the only way to avoid transferring oppositions between employees and employers to firms and workers' dissatisfaction with the government.

Since 2004, while keeping the flexibility of labor market, the central government and local governments have made great efforts in improving social protections through legislation, law enforcement, minimum wage, wage guidelines, and other labor market institutions, as well as the social security system. Western countries always try to find a panacea that simultaneously solves the flexibility and security of the labor market — they even invented the compound word "flexicurity." China's practice is very successful because the labor relations have, so far, been in control. China's experience is acknowledged by the world and has the advantage of backwardness in institutions building.

Compared to western countries, China is more capable of controlling and attaining positive results through building a collective bargaining system of wage and working condition within its current framework. Through the institutions in which unions represent workers, entrepreneur associations coordinate, negotiate, and represent firms and the government guides, China can search for a pattern of labor relations with Chinese characteristics and form harmonious labor relations, which is sustainable, supports intergrowth and co-prosperity, and shares the fruits of development between both firms and workers.

1.3. Extended Reading: Demographic Transition, Demographic Dividend, and Lewis Turning Point in China

Abstract: The disagreements on the changed stages of demographic transition and the role of a demographic dividend in a dual economy development process often lead to wide debates among scholars about China's development stages. This section tries to reveal the nexus between demographic transition and dual economy development: the common starting point, close related processes, and identical characteristics of stages. Based on the empirical evidence of population dynamics, this section supports the judgment of diminishing demographic dividends and an imminent Lewis turning point in China. It also argues that further economic growth, thus faster entry into a high-income economy, is the key and only way to close the "aging before affluence" gap. Accordingly, the section concludes by proposing measures to exploit the potential of the first demographic dividend, creating conditions for a second demographic dividend, and tapping new sources of economic growth.

Introduction

One of the current topics that inspire heated debates among scholars, policy researchers, and even policy-makers is whether Chinese economic growth is losing its source and momentum from demographic dividends. Another related topic is whether or not China will reach its Lewis turning point — namely, labor supply is no longer unlimited. In a research paper, Cai and Wang (2005) estimate that the decline in the population dependence ratio, as a proxy for demographic dividend, contributed 26.8% to per capita GDP growth from 1982 to 2000, and warns that such a demographic dividend will disappear after 2013, when the dependence ratio stops decreasing and begins increasing. By examining changes in the population age structure, labor demand trends, widespread labor shortages, wage rises of ordinary workers, Cai (2008a, 2008b) asserts that the Lewis turning point has indeed arrived, and points out its policy implications in terms of growth pattern transformation, income distribution trends, labor market institutional construction, and human capital accumulation.

While some researchers, and even some policy documents, support and cite the conclusion about the arrival of the Lewis turning point, others strongly disagree. In previous replies, Cai (2008a) tried to provide a wide range of evidence to defend his arguments. It turns out that many people have conflicting opinions about economic reality and explain the same phenomenon in different ways. Many still firmly hold to the conventional wisdom that there is a massive and increasing working-age population, thus an endless surplus labor force in rural areas, and that this is an unchangeable characteristic of China. Propositions which assert the possibility of labor shortage or disappearance of the surplus labor force in agriculture, namely that the Lewis turning point is arriving, are not widely agreed upon.[1] Specifically, all skeptical and critical comments on the judgment about an ongoing Lewis turning point, which result from a static understanding of population and labor force in China, are generally puzzled by the Chinese statistics. In what follows, I will attempt to unveil some aspects of such statistical puzzles.

First, given that the official survey on the utilization of agricultural workforce is unable to reflect the fast changing reality of agricultural production, some scholars are unaware of the changed situation, while others

---

[1] This existing paper does not intend to discuss the divarication that is caused by different definitions of Lewis turning point. According to Lewis (1972) and Ranis and Fei (1961), Lewis turning point can be referred to as the period of time at which expansion of labor demand exceeds that of labor supply and, as a result, wage rate of ordinary workers starts to rise, while wage of agricultural sector is not yet determined by its marginal productivity of labor and the difference of marginal productivity of labor between agricultural and non-agricultural sectors remains. And the time when the wage rates in agricultural and non-agricultural sectors are both determined by their marginal productivity of labor and the gap in productivities disappears can be called commercial point. Only at this time, dual economy ends.

who have tried to understand these statistics are actually trapped in "the tyranny of numbers," as Young (1994) was when he tried to challenge the "East Asian miracle." Either case makes any endeavor of econometric analysis a hostage to the data. The point is that economic reform in China has been too fast for the statistical system to catch up (Ravallion and Chen, 1999). One of the many examples that cause confusion concerns the accurate numbers of agricultural workforce actually used. In 2008, the reported total labor force engaged in agriculture was 307 million, accounting for 39.6% of the country's total employment, and the figure provided by 2008 Agricultural Census was even higher. However, the actual input of labor in agricultural production, calculated based on agricultural costs survey data, turns out to be much less than any published aggregated figures (Cai and Wang, 2008). Taking into consideration the changing trend of the working-age population in rural areas, the updated figure of labor migration from rural to urban sectors, and the extent to which agriculture is mechanized, it must be concluded that the workforce in agricultural production that was actually used is much less than what official statistical publications declare. Therefore, the declaration that there is a large amount of surplus labor to be shifted from agriculture (e.g., Lau, 2010a) and the econometric estimation of marginal productivity of labor in agriculture (e.g., Minami and Ma, 2009), which are both based on the aggregated dataset, tend to overestimate the degree of labor surplus in agriculture and conclude that the Lewis turning point has not come to China.

Second, scholars have difficulties interpreting statistics on the labor market and rural and urban employment, and thus they often elicit inaccurate conclusions. As the result of sectoral changes and increasing diversification of ownership, especially after the labor market shock in the late 1990s, multifaceted sectors have appeared to absorb labor into urban areas, contrary to the pre-reform period when state and collective sectors dominated employment absorption. Among those sectors of employment, large-scale informal employment, the byproduct of reemployment of the laid-off and of the diversity of employment, is new to China. Meanwhile, massive numbers of rural laborers have transformed their jobs from agricultural to non-agricultural sectors, amounting to 240 million, of which 145 million migrated into cities. In routine statistics, neither the informal employment of urban residents nor the employment of migrant workers in urban sectors has been authoritatively reported, except for estimated figures of migrant workers based on sampling surveys and an aggregated estimate of informally employed urban residents under certain assumptions (Cai, 2004). We can view the difference between the number of total employment based on the unit reporting system and the number of employment based on the household survey as a proxy for urban informal employment, which amounts to 95.1 million and accounts for 31.5% of the total urban employment in 2008. This, however, is useless if one wants to do any statistical analysis on structural characteristics of the total employment, because of its lack of disaggregated data. Moreover, the statistical authority has, so far, not promulgated an alternative surveyed unemployment rate data series to the discredited registered unemployment rate, which leads scholars to assume various guesstimates on the unemployment rate. Based on incomplete employment data and unfounded guesstimates, Chinese and international scholars often deduced conclusions, such as zero growth of employment and a high and increasing unemployment rate, (Ru *et al.*, 2008, p. 22; Rawski, 2001; Solinger, 2001) and doubt the authenticity of the widespread labor shortage.

Third, there is no officially published systematic data and up-to-date information on the status of demographic change and population dynamics. While various rounds of national population censuses provide information about population changes, due to a lack of consensus on some important parameters of China's demographics, such as the actual total fertility rate (TFR),[2] no authoritative projections of population change, including predictions of magnitude and the age structure of the population, have been periodically publicized. Therefore, the public and academia do not have updated information about population development trends and many conceive that the peak of population growth will be

---

[2] The 5th National Population Census conducted in 2000 shows that China's TFR was 1.32, which is even lower than policy allowable level of 1.51. Many doubt such a result (e.g., Yu, 2002). Since then, the debates on what is the actual TFR of China have existed among scholars and policy researchers. Generally speaking, the government departments responsible for implementing the population control policy tend to believe a higher TFR, whereas scholars believe a lower TFR. In spite of the disagreement, the estimates mostly fall in the range of 1.6 to 1.8, which are all significantly lower than the replacement level of 2.1.

reached in or after 2040, then the total population in China will be as high as 1.6 billion (e.g., Lau, 2010b). More specifically, most scholars ignore the fact that the growth of China's working-age population has slowed, thus the demographic foundation of unlimited labor supply has shrunk, and therefore they are unwilling to accept the assertion of an ongoing Lewis turning point associated with a diminishing demographic dividend.

It is obvious that an undistorted understanding of demographic transition statuses and trends will help scholars and policy researchers better understand the state of the labor market and will serve as a foundation for policy decisions on how China can sustain its economic growth. The following sections argue that, to a large extent, demographic transition and dual economy development have a common starting point, related and similar characteristics of development stages, as well as overlapping processes, so that the demographic window of opportunity in which a demographic dividend is obtained is one of the stages of dual economy development. Accordingly, the theoretical and empirical work and reasoning of a diminishing demographic dividend and incoming Lewis turning point solve this problem in a single action. The rest of the paper is organized as follows: The second section reveals a stylized fact about the relationship between demographic transition and dual economy development based on international experiences; the third section depicts China's process of demographic transition and its impact on economic growth; the fourth section tries to answer the question of how the "aging before affluence" gap can be narrowed; and the last section concludes by drawing policy implications of the issues discussed in the paper.

Stages of Demographic Transition and Development of Dual Economy

The theory of dual economy, coined by Lewis (1954), divides a typical developing economy into two sectors: the agricultural and modern sectors. Because labor force is not relative to capital and land in agriculture, its marginal productivity in the sector is very low, even as low as zero or below. As the modern sector expands, the surplus labor in agriculture is transferred to the modern sector without a substantial rise of wages. This whole process is typically called the development of a dual economy. Such a process continues until it reaches a point at which the growth of labor demand exceeds the growth of labor supply and further labor transfer requires an increase in unskilled workers' wage rate. That point is generally called the Lewis turning point. In spite of its fluctuations in economics history (Ranis, 2004), the Lewisian theory of dual economy has always remained an important theoretical model of development economics.

Even before Lewis's prominent paper first appeared, the mature form of demographic transition theory had already been published.[3] Corresponding to pre- and post-industrialization periods, demographic transition is categorized into three stages, which are respectively characterized by (1) high birth rate, high death rate, and low natural growth rate of a population; (2) high birth rate, low death rate, and high natural growth rate of a population; and (3) low birth rate, low death rate, and low natural growth rate of a population. Although we cannot judge whether Lewis noticed those literatures in demography, there is no lack of demographic assumptions related to the theory of demographic transition in his description of dual economy development. While defining the unlimited supply of labor, which is the key concept of the theory of dual economy, he explains: "Unlimited supply of labor may be said to exist in those countries where population is so large, relatively, to capital and natural resources, that there are large sectors of the economy where the marginal productivity of labor is negligible, zero, or even negative." The connotative assumption of this statement is that a typical dual economy characterized by an unlimited supply of labor is at the second stage of demographic transition — that is, natural growth rate of a population is high as the result of declined mortality and inertial high birth rate. Since agriculture is the primary sector in the sectoral chain, it is the first place where the abundant population and surplus labor force settle.

---

[3] Whereas Thompson (1929) first identified the three stages of demographic transition and another scholar added two more later stages, they were both not considered as the father of theory of demographic transition, because they did not provide standard theoretical explanation on decline of fertility. The honor was later awarded to Notestein (1945). Please see Caldwell (1976) for a brief history of this field.

The key to comprehending the logical and empirical relationship between demographic transition and development of dual economy is to explore how the demographic dividend is engendered and obtained. In the early literature of demography and economics, the population-development nexus was discussed by focusing on the relationship between economic growth rate and population growth rate or population quantum, while the discussion on demographic transition was mainly about demographic contents, such as population quantity, birth rate, and death rate, but not closely related to economic growth. Besides, the growth theory mainstream, while incorporating population into endogenous growth, usually neglects the characteristics of dual economy demographic transition. After a long period of neglect of economic development and structural characteristics of population, particularly the relationship between population age structure and labor supply, as all developed countries and many newly industrialized economies successively completed their demographic transition process, demographers became conscious of population aging and its consequences. Economists further unveiled the change in working-age population along with fertility decline and its effect on economic growth sources (Williamson, 1997). That is, in the interval between an increasing death rate decline and decreasing birth rate decline, the natural growth rate of a population is usually at its fastest rise, so youth dependence ratio is also increasing. After a certain period of time, as fertility decreases and as the "baby boomers" enter adulthood, the proportion of working-age population enhances accordingly. The further decline in fertility as a result of economic and social developments causes a deceleration of a population's natural growth rate, and the structural consequence of such a dynamic is population aging. In short, following a reversed U-shaped pattern, namely, the natural growth rate of a population first increases and then declines after a turning point, with an interval of about one generation, the growth rate of the working-age population presents a similar pattern of changes.

During the period in which population age structure is most productive, an adequate supply of labor and a high savings rate afford an extra source of economic growth, thus forming demographic dividend. Consequently, once demographic transition exceeds this stage, namely, population age structure becomes less and less productive because of rapid aging, such a conventionally defined demographic dividend gradually disappears. Since the stages in demographic transition can be sufficiently characterized by changes in the total fertility rate (TFR), one can theoretically expect the following relationship between demographic transition and economic growth (Figure 1.1): the stage of high TFR coincides with steady state of low growth rate; as TFR falls and, as a result, a more productive population age structure comes into being, demographic dividend promotes economic growth to a higher rate; when TFR further drops to a low level and the population ages, economic growth rate shrinks again to low steady state. Correspondingly, at a certain stage of demographic transition when TFR rapidly declines and population age structure becomes more and more productive, a demographic window of opportunity forms.

It is worth noting that factors impacting the performance of economic growth are multifold, not just of population. This is also true in explaining both the steady growth rate of low income economies, known for its poverty trap, and the steady growth rate of high-income economies struggling in technological innovation frontier. For example, in the empirical works that defend neoclassical growth theory, economists have found more than

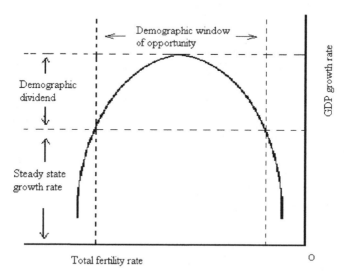

Figure 1.1.   Relationship between Fertility and Economic Growth.

one hundred explanatory variables, which are statistically significant in unveiling determinants of growth performances, but none is sufficient and exclusive (Sala-i-Martin, 1997). In other words, we also put aside the retroaction effect of economic growth on demographic transition[4] and focus on the straightforward relationship between fertility and economic growth. Under the assumption made above, this fertility–growth nexus can be deduced from the theory of demographic dividend and confirmed empirically.

The panel data from World Development Indicators enable us to picture a descriptive relationship between annual GDP growth rates and TFR levels among countries in the period between 1960 to recent years. For those countries and years, for which data is available, annual GDP growth rates ranged from −51% to 106%. To avoid the complication of explaining the outliers, we ignore those extreme numbers and only investigate those between 0% and 10%, which is assumed to be the normal span of annual GDP growth rate. According to foregoing discussions, the relationship between economic growth rate and fertility is not a simple linear relationship, but follows an algebraic relationship of a quadratic function. That is, as TFR declines, the economic growth rate first increases and then declines. In Figure 1.2, according to the function relations between GDP growth rate and TFR and the square term of TFR, we present the fitted value of annual growth rate of GDP with 95% confidence interval.

Figure 1.2 intuitively pictures a reversed U-shaped pattern of GDP growth rate against the decline in TFR. Countries at the lower stage of demographic transition, characterized by high TFR, usually suffer poor economic performance, but as their TFR levels fall, economic growth speeds up. After a certain point, as TFR further declines and demographic transition enters the later stage characterized by very low TFR, economic growth tends to slow. Such a simplified empirical curve is perfectly consistent with the theoretical prediction described previously. To further examine the statistical significance of the relationship between TFR and

---

[4] In an econometric study, Du (2004) found that population policy, per capita GDP, and level of human capital are decisive factors driving down China's fertility and empirically identified the different effects of the three factors.

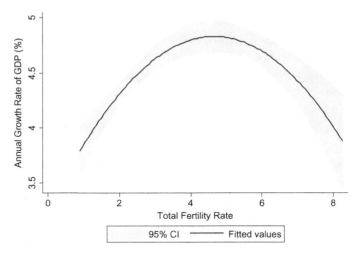

Figure 1.2.   Empirical Relationship between TFR and GDP Growth.
Source: Calculation based on dataset of *World Development Indicators*.

Table 1.1.   Regression Results: The Relation between TFR and Growth.

	Coefficient	**Standard error**	*t*-**value**	**$P > \mid t \mid$**
TFR	0.6852	0.1133	6.05	0.000
TFR square	−0.0736	0.0137	−5.38	0.000
Constant term	3.2359	0.1909	16.95	0.000
Observations		3380		

economic growth, by assuming the nonlinear correlation and using fore-going data, we regress GDP growth rate on TFR and the squared term of TFR (Table 1.1). The regression results show the reverse U-shaped relationship between GDP growth and TFR by revealing the significantly positive sign of TFR coefficient and negative sign of the squared term of TFR.

While the more precise explanation, based on both economics theory and empirical evidence, requires much more works, the plain fertility–growth nexus here is a sufficient framework. We are now in the position of investigating actual relations between demographic transition perceived in demography, demographic dividend coined by demographic economists, and Lewis turning point deduced from development economics, based on China's experiences. In the next section, we will analyze the formation and anticipated disappearance of demographic dividend, and conclude the advent of the Lewis turning point in the process of China's economic development.

The economic impacts of Chinese demographic transition

In the first two decades after the establishment of the People's Republic of China in 1949, the economy rapidly recovered and people's living standards greatly improved, which pushed China's demographic transition into the second stage. That is, eliminating the abnormal years between the late 1950s and early 1960s, mortality fell substantially, birth rate remained at a chronic height, and, as a result, natural growth rate was constantly high. TFR had kept as high as six until the 1970s, and afterward, it declined dramatically. However, the fastest decline of TFR had occurred before the one-child policy was formally implemented. TFR dropped by 3.5 percentage points, from 5.8% to 2.3% in the decade between 1970 to 1980, while it dropped by 0.5 to 0.7 percentage point in the entire period between 1980 — in which the central government announced a compulsory population control policy — and the present day, when TFR is agreed to be between 1.6 to 1.8, which are both well below the replacement level. Such a fact shows that the orderly switchover of major stages of demographic transition is primarily the result of economic growth and social development. In the period of demographic transition from the second to third stages, population at the working age grows faster than dependent population, therefore the proportion of the working-age population becomes increasingly larger, which has released demographic dividend and upgraded economic growth rate to a level above a steady state.

Although the population dependence ratio, namely, the ratio of dependent population aged 14 years and younger and 65 years and older, to working-age population aged 15 to 64 years, declined as early as the mid-1960s, the substantial increase in the working-age population and its share in the total population, associated by dramatic fall of population dependence ratio, began in the mid-1970s (Figure 1.3). Such a favorable age

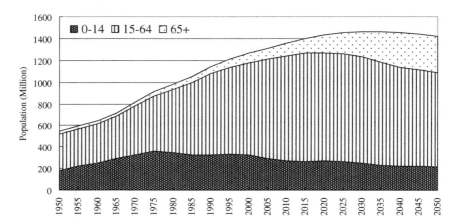

Figure 1.3.   Changing Trends of Age Structure of Population.
Source: United Nations (2009).

structure of population has been translated into a demographic dividend that spurred unprecedented performance of economic growth. A series of publications (e.g., Cai, 2008; Cai and Wang, 2005) explain the rationale, process, and empirics of the demographic dividend in the development of dual economy of China. Those studies also argue that as such a dividend begins diminishing at the demographic transition stage, characterized by low birth rate, low mortality, and low growth rate of population, when the development of the Chinese dual economy has reached its critical period of time, the Lewis turning point. This section is an endeavor in synthesizing demographic transition, demographic dividend, and Lewis turning point, accounting for the logical and historical relations between the three concepts and revealing the challenges facing the Chinese economy in a changing era.

The prediction of China's population and its age composition by the United Nations (2009), shown in Figure 1.3, is a scenario of medium variant and is consistent with the 2000 census, the 2005 sample census, and updated (to 2008) estimates of the subsequent trends in fertility, mortality, and international migration. This prospect is by and large identical to those made by various Chinese units. According to this prediction, the total population of China is going to reach its peak in 2030, at 1.46 billion people. Much sooner than that, the working-age population, aged 15 to 64 years, will reach its peak in 2015, at 998 million people. Although such prospects can be obtained from public sources, it is obvious that they are unknown information, not only the public but also to many economists. To acquaint oneself of the changing trends of the Chinese population is definitely required for the scholars who are studying and speaking of the future of the Chinese economic development, and influencing the public.

Further examining the prediction results shown in Figure 1.3, one can find that the growth speed of the working-age population has been faster than that of the total population between 1970 to 2010, and the trend will turn the other way around, namely, the age structure of the Chinese population will be no longer evolved to be productive. As the agricultural share of labor force declines over time, the current demand of urban sectors for labor has been sufficiently met by rural-to-urban migration. As an important part of the reform, opening-up, and growth in the past 30 years, the massive migration has drawn worldwide attention and been recognized as the largest movement of population in history during a time of peace (Roberts *et al.*, 2004). In recent years, as a result of the long-standing adjustment corresponding to migration, two new phenomena to the labor relocation have occurred. First, as mechanization of agricultural production has increasingly accelerated, migrant workers continually become unwanted. Second, as a result of the shrinkage of local urban labor force, the demand of urban sectors for migrant workers becomes increasingly rigid and indispensable (Cai, 2010).

According to another prediction, which takes into account the impacts of rural-to-urban migration (Hu, 2009), by 2015, the amount of incremental working-age population in urban areas will be less than that of reduced working-age population in rural areas (Figure 1.4), which is the same conclusion drawn by the above cited prediction. This prediction implies that, without substantial enhancement of wages and other incentives, the migrant workers will not fill up the gap vacated by the rapid reduction of urban labor force. In the course of urbanization, the migrant workers and their accompanying family members who live in urban areas for more than six months are already counted as urban residents, so the number of statistically recognized rural residents has been rapidly reduced. The labor market has gradually responded to this situation, which is embodied both

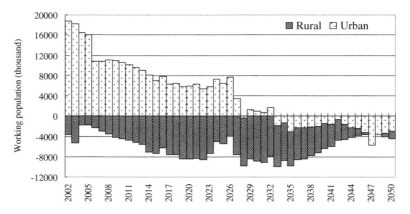

Figure 1.4. Changes of Working-Age Population of Rural and Urban China.
Source: Hu (2009).

in the tremendous enhancement of wages of ordinary workers and in the nationwide labor shortage. According to the definition of development economics, those phenomena are signals of the Lewis turning point.

How to close the "aging before affluence" gap

Worldwide experiences show that economic growth and social development are major driving forces of demographic transition, while the implementation of population policy plays a relatively minor role to the former. Like China, the economies of Asian countries such as Korea, Singapore, Thailand, and Taiwan, where no compulsory policy has been enforced, have experienced dramatic decline in fertility, from high TFR similar to China in the 1950s, to as low as below-replacement levels in the 1990s. Even in India, where economic growth and social development have not performed as well as China and those economies, demographic transition has been relatively lagging behind, and fertility has also been declining by following the similar path (Lin, 2006).

In spite of its unprecedented economic growth in the past 30 years, due to its late outset compared to the Asian economies mentioned previously, China entered into the new stage of demographic transition at a relatively low income per capita, which is characterized by "aging before affluence." In 2000, the proportion of the population age 65 years and over in China's total population was 6.8%, identical to the world average, whereas China's per capita GNI was only 17.3% of the world average based on the official exchange rate and 56.3% of the world average based on the purchasing power parity. While one must admit that the strict implementation of the one-child policy accelarates decline of the fertility rate, the demographic transition, in the final analysis, is the result of outstanding economic growth and social development (Du, 2004). The difference in income level between China and developed countries is therefore the root cause of the existing "aging before affluence" gap.

Most developed countries are facing the challenges of an aging population to sustainable economic growth and pension insurance plans, and the efforts and effects vary from country to country. However, the developed countries, being at a high-income level, are of the technological innovation frontier, and therefore with increasing productivity, have dealt well with the challenges and have so far averted the old-age crisis. Based on experiences, one can be confident that China's key to tackling the challenges of a shrinking working-age population and enhancing the elderly population is to sustain its fast economic growth and quick increase in per capita income. In other words, demographic transition, and thus population aging, is an irreversible process, which cannot be stopped even if the one-child policy is abolished. The already formed "aging before affluence" gap can only be narrowed and eventually closed by catching up with developed countries, which puts China in the ranks of high-income countries.

As China ascends into the world's economy and has already become the second largest economy after the U.S., given its decreased population growth rate, the per capita GDP level of China rapidly increases. One long-term prediction on China's economic size and per capita GDP conducted by Japanese Center for Economic Research (JCER, 2007) shows that, based on PPP and the constant USD of 2000, China's GDP volume will reach 17.3 trillion USD in 2020, 25.2 trillion USD in 2030, and 30.4 trillion USD in 2040. The predicted per capita GDP in the three reference years are 12,000 USD, 18,000 USD, and 22,000 USD, respectively. An even more optimistic prediction by Fogel (2007) expects that China's total GDP will reach 123.7 trillion USD in 2040, and, based on the predicted population of 1.46 billion, per capita GDP will then be as high as 85,000 USD. Those two prospects are widely divergent in terms of methodology, data usage, assumptions, and, therefore, the predicted results. Given the debatable usage of the purchasing power parity GDP term by both researches, their prospects are unlikely to be accepted by Chinese scholars and officials.

The above-mentioned are controversial prospects on China's economic volume and per capita income; however, China will increase its transformation from a middle-income country to a high-income country during the second decade of the 21st century, making China's economy the second largest in the world. Suppose China can maintain the same, or even appreciably lower growth rates of both total and per capita GDP realized in the past 30 years, a significant convergence of wealth between China and developed countries will be realized. In this regard, the predictions made by foreign economists reflect the correct direction and vision of the near future, and, as a result of these trends, under the assumption of unchanged demographic transition, the gap between economic development level and population aging will eventually be closed.

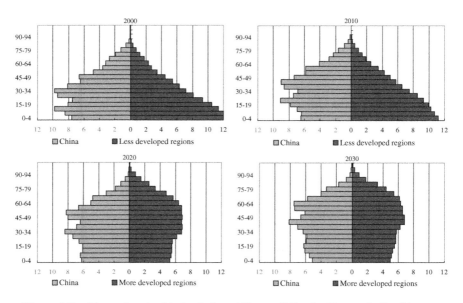

Figure 1.5. Narrowing the "Aging before Affluence" Gap by Economic Catching up.
Source: United Nations (2009).

In Figure 1.5, we compare China's age structure of population with less-developed countries in the years of 2000 and 2010 to show the characteristic of "aging before affluence," whereas we compare China's age structure of population with more-developed countries in the years of 2020 to 2030 to show how the "aging before affluence" gap can be narrowed and finally closed. This shows that the fundamental avenues to dealing with population aging in the post-Lewis turning point era are threefold: (1) tap the potential of remaining demographic dividend; (2) create second demographic dividend; and (3) find new sources sustaining long-run economic growth.

Conclusion and policy implications

The analysis on China's demographic transition and its economic impacts convince us of the close relationship between demographic transition and economic development, and thus the conclusion of the diminishing demographic dividend and the ongoing Lewis turning point is pursuable with both economic theory and empirical evidence. Even the scorching debates around those judgments, to some extent, suggest that they are not solely academic discussions, but that they also have important implications to policy decision.

The arrival of the Lewis turning point is a vital milestone for a developing economy, because only by passing through this point can the marginal productivity of labor in traditional (agricultural) sector begin to converge in modern (non-agricultural) sectors. When eventually the productivity gap among sectors disappears, the economy as a whole receives its commercial point and the long-standing dual economy terminates. Therefore, the advent of the Lewis turning point is not dismal news at all. On the contrary, being cognizant of this turning point not only has theoretical meaning, but also practical significance. That is, it has important implications for governments in development policy formation, for enterprises in decision-making, and for individuals in adjustment in the face of labor market changes. In short, the sustainability of economic growth relies heavily on a sound response to the challenges brought forward by the new stage of development. What follows is our examination of the potential sources of China's sustained economic growth in the post-Lewis turning point period, based on experiences of foregoer economies.

First, there still is potential for the existing demographic dividend to develop in the short term. Let us first divide demographic dividend into two types: first demographic dividend and second demographic dividend. While the first demographic dividend can be defined as the scenario where labor supply is adequate and savings rate is high, thanks to the increasing magnitude and proportion of the working-age population, the second demographic dividend can be seen as the new motivation of savings resulted from precautions for the elderly and new supply of human capital supposedly brought about by postponing retirement age and extending education and training (Cai, 2009). The exploitation of the first demographic dividend has been manifested in labor transformation from agricultural to secondary and tertiary sectors, accompanied by speedy urbanization. By 2009, the number of urban residents who lived in cities for six months or longer reached more than 600 million, accounting for 46% of the Chinese population. While according to the definition, only part of these migrants were counted as urbanites, because they do not legitimately have urban *hukou* and lack access to public services, of which urban residents with local *hukou* are inherently privileged, they are not fully urbanized.

More specifically, because migrant workers and their accompanied families still expect to return home to rural areas periodically, especially during the Chinese New Year period, and permanently after they are not needed by the urban labor market, (1) their supply of labor is not durative, (2) their consumption behavior is still rural, (3) they are not planned for the utilization of urban infrastructure, and (4) they have no incentives to contribute to the social security scheme, particularly to the fully-funded pension system. In 2007, the proportion of urban residents to the total Chinese population, which includes those migrant workers who live in cities for more than six months, was 45%, whereas the proportion of the population who have formal urban *hukou* was only 33%, which leaves a 12-percentage-point gap between nominal and actual urbanization rates. By transforming farmers-turned-workers to migrants-turned-citizens through deepening the *hukou* reform and equalizing public services to all citizens, a more complete urbanization can make full use of the first demographic dividend (Cai, 2010).

Second, there is potential for the second demographic dividend to be tapped in the medium term. An aging society can also possess population advantage, namely the second demographic dividend, as long as necessary institutional conditions are provided (Lee and Mason, 2006; Cai, 2009). As one of the important causes for population aging, the increase in life expectancy (people living longer and healthier) is the foundation to generate the second demographic dividend. This kind of demographic dividend includes three major sources. The first source comes from the need of old-age supports and supply of pension institutions. As long as there is a fully funded pension scheme instead of a pay-as-you-go or family support system, the older and longer-working workforce will have a larger incentive to accumulate assets, and the high savings rate can be maintained by investing in capital market (Lee and Mason, 2006). A second source comes from the expansion of education resources. As the quantity of the young population reduces and its proportion in total population declines, the capacity of the working-age population to maintain at school relatively enhances, which is a window of opportunity for extending education and training, hence accumulate human capital. A third source comes from the expansion of labor force participation. Extension of the retirement age is a major measure to enlarge the workforce and alleviate the burden of old-age supports, which is widely employed in developed countries. For China, the obstacle of extending retirement age is that the working elderly are usually less educated and thus unwanted by employers. Before this situation is changed, the extension of retirement age may put them in a vulnerable circumstance. Therefore, the exploitation of such a dividend should take a gradual approach through expanding education, especially that at a senior-high-school-level liberal education, occupational education, and on-job-training, particularly for migrant workers.

Third, there is a great need to obtain a brand new driving force for the sustainable economic growth through growth pattern transformation in the long run. Assuming scarcity of labor and thus diminishing returns to capital, the neoclassical theory of growth developed based on western experiences argues that the only way to maintain the sustained economic growth is to enhance the contributive share of total factor productivity (TFP) to it (for example, Solow, 1956). Based on this basic assumption, a handful of studies doubted the existence of the "East Asian miracle" and, if there is, its sustainability (e.g., Young, 1992; Krugman, 1994). In reality, thanks partially to the characteristics of unlimited supply of labor and partially to felicitous economic policies favorable for exploiting demographic dividend, the East Asian economies had long averted the crisis of diminishing return of capital. As some major economies passed through their Lewis turning points,[5] at the same time, the newly entered stage of demographic transition no longer provided first demographic dividend. Those economies represented by Japan and the "Four Asian Tigers" transformed their economic growth pattern from capital and labor driven to more TFP driven. Those experiences indicate that as the first demographic dividend diminishes and Lewis turning point passes through, driving forces of the Chinese economic growth will eventually be transformed to a reliance on technological advancement and productivity enhancement. The assurance of the changed stage of development requires an increase in the pace of growth pattern transformation.

---

[5]It is commonly believed that the Japanese economy in 1960 and Korean and Taiwan economies reached their Lewis turning point, respectively (e.g., Minami, 1968; Bai, 1982).

Chapter 2

The Disappearance of Demographic Dividends

2.1. How China is Dealing with the Problem of "Growing Old Before Becoming Rich"

Predictions of China's population are usually based on the total fertility rate (TFR; namely, the number of children borne by a woman during her life span) of 1.8, which has been reportedly unchanged over the past 20 years. This number is no longer accurate, as the calculated TFR has been lower than 1.5 for many years, according to the data published by the National Statistics Bureau. In the 2009 World Population Policies published by the United Nations, China's TFR was modified to 1.4 in 2006, categorizing China as part of the low fertility rate countries.

The result of having a low fertility rate is that China's population is aging and the growth of the working-age population is decreasing. According to the United Nations' median age prediction, the increment of China's working-age population will gradually decrease and become zero between 2000 and 2015. Meanwhile, the proportion of elderly population above 65 years old will increase from 6.8% to 9.6% and the elderly population will exceed 130 million.

So far, China's demographic structure is characterized by an abundant and high proportion of working-age population, which ensures sufficient labor supply. It also has the precondition to form a high saving rate, which provides demographic dividends for economic growth since the reform and opening-up in the early 1980s. Based on our estimates, the decreasing dependency ratio contributed 26.8% of the increase in GDP per capita between 1980 and 2000. However, according to conservative predictions, dependency ratio in China will stop decreasing and will instead begin to increase in 2013, which implies that demographic dividends from the age advantage will disappear.

It is the general rule that population will gradually age with economic growth and social development. However, it is unusual that China entered the demographic transition period with a large aging population, but at a development level with low income per capita. For example, China's elderly population above 65 years was 8.9% compared to the world average of 7.5% in 2010, while China's GDP per capita in current USD was only 47.7% of the world average level in the same year. In 2013, South Korea and Thailand will experience the lowest dependency ratio, together with China, but in 2010, the GDP per capita in South Korea was four times that of China, and Thailand had a slightly higher income per capita than China. So, the saying "growing old before becoming rich" is more accurate than generally saying that "population is aging" when describing China's demographic challenge.

From the approached demographic transition period, China is gradually losing its comparative advantage of abundant and inexpensive labor supply because of the changes in its demographic age structure. With labor shortage and increasing labor cost, China's labor-intensive manufacturing products will become less competitive. In the meantime, China does not have enough comparative advantage for competition in capital-intensive and technology-intensive industries at the current economic growth level. As an open economy, China is not only a typical middle-income country but it also faces the dangers of the middle-income trap. However, many pioneers, especially the East Asian economies, have enough experience to overcome the middle-income trap by choosing the right development strategy. Therefore, China still has the advantage of backwardness in technology and can deal with the problem of "growing old before becoming rich," as well as avoiding the middle-income trap, from existing experiences and lessons.

First of all, it is urgent for China to transition to the productivity-driven economic growth pattern. In the neoclassical economic growth theory, economic growth is sustainable only if the total factor productivity increases continually with the assumptions of limited labor supply and diminishing marginal returns to capital. The theory is challenged in understanding the source of economic growth in East Asia and China in the period with demographic dividend. These economies once had the dual-economy structure with unlimited labor supply, which violated the assumptions above. However, China's economy now has more characteristics of the neoclassical economic growth since its population is aging. Besides, its economic growth cannot be sustained in the pattern that relies only on expanding inputs, but without increasing the total factor productivity.

Economists agree that Japan was trapped in "The Lost Decade" (or even two decades) because of insufficient growth of total factor productivity after its demographic dividends disappeared in the early 1990s. If Japan fell into the "high-income trap" because of the long-term economic growth stagnation, China will fall into the "middle-income trap" in following the same route. However, China still has huge potential to improve total factor productivity and increase its contribution to economic growth with efforts in the following aspects: to improve workers' skills and upgrade industries; to remove institutional barriers for labor migration and resource reallocation; to transform government functions and reform the investment and financial system; and to increase firms' overall efficiency through competition, etc.

Second, China should speed up the transition to the consumption-driven economic growth pattern. Increasing domestic demand is an important method to maintaining sustainable economic growth in the period when traditional comparative advantage is diminishing and new comparative advantage is insignificant. It is imperative that China increase consumption in order to improve national income distribution and basic public services in primary distribution and redistribution areas. As labor shortage becomes a more widespread phenomenon, the average workers' wages are continually increasing, which provides the precondition to improve income distribution. However, experiences all over the world show that income distribution will not be improved spontaneously, unless corresponding labor market institutions and social protection mechanisms are developed.

China's current stage of development necessitates the acceleration of the formation of labor market institutions in the primary distribution area, especially to increase wages as labor productivity rises through the collective wage bargaining system. In the redistribution area, China should emphasize on increasing the social security coverage rate of peasant workers. Although peasant workers' wages increased quickly and their working conditions have significantly improved in recent years, their basic social security coverage rate is still low. For example, retirement insurance coverage rate, unemployment insurance coverage rate, and basic medical insurance coverage rate of peasant workers were only 9.8%, 3.7%, and 13.1% in 2009. One important institutional reason for the insufficient social protection for peasant workers is the separation of the urban and rural household registration systems. Peasant workers and their families in urban areas are not registered as urban residents. They have high mobility to migrate between rural and urban areas and are usually left out of the social security system. Therefore, reform of the household registration system for the urbanization of peasant workers should accelerate.

Additionally, China should adjust its population policy with the times. Although the demographic structure changes with economic growth and social development, and the trend of population aging is irreversible, there are three sufficient reasons for China to adjust the childbearing policy while adhering to its basic family planning policy.

First of all, there exists space to achieve future demographic equilibrium through policy adjustments. Surveys on fertility desires show that each Chinese couple desires 1.7 children on average. Specifically, each Chinese couple desired 1.74, 1.70, and 1.73 children on average in 1997, 2001, and 2006, respectively. However, the fertility rate policy (i.e., the average number of children allowed per family) is 1.5, while the actual total fertility rate is 1.4. There is an obvious difference between policy-determined fertility rate and real fertility desires.

Second, the "one-child" policy has successfully accomplished its goal as per expectations. When officially declaring the policy in 1980, Chinese Communist Party Central Committee announced that "a different population policy can be applied when the particularly intensive population growth problem is relieved in 30 years." Currently, the condition for "applying a different population policy" is much more mature than expected. Therefore, there is sufficient evidence to validate policy adjustments.

Third, practices of local policy adjustments provide the blueprint and road map for the reform. Most provinces currently have allowed that for families with both parents, the "only child" can have two children (commonly referred as the "double only-child" policy). This policy adjustment has not significantly affected the fertility rate. Following this route, once it moves to the point that for families with only one parent, the "only child" can have two children ("single only-child" policy), the policy adjustment will cover a larger portion of the population and perhaps can affect the long term demographic equilibrium.

2.2. How China Responds to the Disappearance of Demographic Dividends

Since China has benefited from demographic dividends for a long time, many people predict that this source of economic growth will disappear around 2013 as the dependency ratio stops decreasing. There are different opinions toward this finding in both academic and policy analysis areas. It is unusual to see such a huge difference, deep opposition, and intense emotion in an academic debate. It is similar to the traditional opposition between optimists and pessimists in the field of economics after the economist Thomas Robert Malthus published *An Essay on the Principle of Population*. However, in my opinion, both parties in the debate on whether China's demographic dividends will disappear are pessimists. It will be explained in this section. This section will also answer how China deals with the disappearance of demographic dividends.

The origin of demographic dividends

The concept and popularity of demographic dividends has only existed for a short time. In the 1990s, when applying the econometric model to explain East Asia's miracle of Japan and the "Four Tigers" in Asia, as well as the historical economic growth in the new continent exceeding that in Europe, some economists from Harvard University found that the dependency ratio — namely, the ratio of dependent population to working-age population significantly contributed to the economic growth, with dependency ratio as an independent variable. Such a non-traditional production factor that contributes to the economic growth is called demographic dividends.

Applying similar assumptions and econometric methods to China's economic growth since the reform and opening-up, we find that the growth rate of GDP per capita will increase by 0.115% as total dependency ratio decreases by 1%. Between 1980 and 2000 (most updated data during our research at the time), the total dependency ratio decreased by 20.1%, when the growth rate of GDP per capita was around 8.6% in the same period. Therefore, the decreasing total dependency ratio contributed 26.8% to the growth rate of GDP per capita. I will give several explanations to clarify this econometric analysis result in the following paragraphs.

First of all, the economic growth process is not as simple as described in the model. If using dependency ratio as the source of demographic dividends, it should have started decreasing in the mid-1960s. However, for rapid economic growth, this demographic advantage cannot be used without other conditions. Only the reform and opening-up provided the favorable conditions to use demographic dividends. More specifically, resources can only be reallocated with labor migration. At the same time, abundant and inexpensive labor resources can be transformed into an additional source of economic growth (demographic dividends) with the precondition that China has integrated into the global economy with the development of labor-intensive manufacturing industries in coastal areas. Therefore, if the reader wants to visualize demographic dividends with an abstract concept in the econometric model, it is best to focus on analyzing the 230 million peasant workers spread all over the country.

Second, the explanatory variable of the model (dependency ratio) reflects the demographic age structure. Rather than its quantity, the focus should be on the trend of changes in the demographic age structure. In other words, it is more important to have a continually increasing working-age population and a higher proportion of this group in the total population, rather than just a large quantity of it. For example, the average growth rate of the population between 15 and 64 years old was 1.8%, with its proportion in the total population increasing from 59.7% to 71% from 1980 to 2005. This caused the dependency ratio to continually decrease and form demographic dividends with an abundant labor supply and high saving rate. If regarding the quantity of the working-age population as demographic dividends, is it a mistake to measure an economic performance by the size of a country?

Third, this conclusion is not related to the reason for the decreasing dependency ratio. Decreasing dependency ratio should be explained with real population changes in the framework of demographic transition theory. China has experienced a much shorter demographic transition process time than what most developed countries experienced for over a hundred years, and entered a new demographic transition period with low birth rate, low mortality rate, and low natural population growth rate in the early 2000s. When natural population growth rate first increased and then decreased, growth rate of the working-age population first rose and then fell similarly. Its rising period occurred when the dependency ratio continually decreased and demographic dividends were gained. It should be pointed out that the main driving force of demographic transition is economic growth and social development, with birth policies only in a supporting role. South Korea, Singapore, and Taiwan Province did not implement any mandatory birth control policy, but experienced decrease in total fertility rate from a similar high starting point in the 1950s, to a below-replacement level of 2.1, like China, after 1990.

Debates from different policy intentions

Due to the published work mentioned earlier and my extension to its policy implications with econometric analysis results, there are always scholars using the concept of demographic dividends to ignite broad debates. Despite non-academic arguments, debates on demographic dividends focus on the aspects mentioned in the following paragraphs.

The first is on whether demographic dividends will disappear. Using dependency ratio as the proxy variable of demographic dividends in our analysis, the assumption that demographic dividends will disappear is a reasonable conclusion, since demographic predictions show that total dependency ratio will rise after 2013. Some scholars think that demographic dividends will not disappear at that time, since the aggregate quantity of the working-age population is still large and the total dependency ratio is predicted to remain low until 2035. From an inaccurate angle, or simply from the aggregate quantity of working-age population,

China's demographic structure will not be gravely damaged by that time. However, this finding is not supported, since the concept of demographic dividends has specific meaning and is estimated from a specific variable. In addition, I remind the reader that the key of demographic dividends is the dynamic changes of working-age population or the dependency ratio. The assertion that demographic dividends will continue to exist is not convincing, since the working-age population will absolutely decrease after 2013 and its proportion in the total population will decrease from 72% to 64% with predicted working-age population decreasing 0.4% annually on average between 2015 and 2035.

The second is on the policy implications of demographic dividends. I have pointed out in the beginning of the section that both parties are actually pessimists, no matter if they agree on the disappearance of demographic dividends, or believe in the continual existence of demographic dividends. My reason is that most people who agree on the disappearance of demographic dividends believe this change will cause China to lose the comparative advantage in labor-intensive manufacturing industries and the economic growth rate that has been maintained over the past 30 years. Even those investment economists who direct investment with the theory of demographic dividends imply that this window of opportunity will close in the future, though advocating that the current demographic age structure can still benefit from investments in the stock market and housing market. In contrast, people who believe in the continual existence of demographic dividends are making all efforts to prove that demographic dividends will not soon disappear, simply because they consider the observed demographic changes to be a big concern.

There are two policy implications of demographic dividends that should be discussed. One is the concern that birth control policy has accomplished its initial goal and needs adjustment once admitting the disappearance of demographic dividends. In fact, there is no necessary relationship, or close causality, between demographic dividends and birth policies. Following our discussion earlier, demographic transition is the result of economic growth and social development. So far, countries and regions that have completed demographic transitions did not implement any birth control policy. Therefore, the adjustment on birth policies will not change the trends of population aging and the disappearance of demographic dividends as far as China's development continues. Observing the following facts helps us to understand that there is no consistency or causality in the time of the three most important phenomenon, i.e., demographic dependency ratio started decreasing in the mid-1960s, total fertility rate significantly decreased between 1970 and 1980, and the "one-child" policy was officially enforced in 1980.

Another concern is that it implies that employment pressure has started and will continue to be relieved once admitting the disappearance of demographic dividends, and people may drop their guard toward employment problems, and even lower the priority of employment in government policies. The logic behind this perception is relevant to the background in which the Chinese government's proactive employment policy was formed, i.e., paying full attention to employment problems was caused by concerns from the severe situation of laid-off workers from large-scale state-owned enterprises in the late 1990s. It appears that this policy will not be necessary if the severe employment situation is relieved. However, the logic connection between them does not exist. Developed market economy countries are always characterized with labor shortage, though their politicians and macroeconomic policy makers give greater attention to employment problems than we do.

The third is on the business or investment implications of demographic dividends. It is commonly seen that the conclusion of economic research attracted the attention of investors and investment analysts as soon as it led to intensive debates in academia. It is the case for the debate on demographic dividends that corporate financial economists and investment analysts, who did not agree on our initial finding, continued using the concept of demographic dividends to widen their investing prospects and did not mind modifying their points of view accordingly. The reason is very simple: they have to take direct responsibility for their investment clients. I described this phenomenon with the poem of Su Shi that "the duck knows first when water becomes warmer in spring."

Marketing demography or business demography is a branch of demography that connects changes in demographic characteristics, as well as consumption and saving behaviors, with investment and innovation opportunities. This analysis indeed helps broaden an investor's view. However, since analyzing the policy implications of demographic dividends can result in a misleading conclusion, there exists the danger of misusing demographic dividends for investment advices, especially when analysts have little knowledge of the economic meanings of demographic transition. The conclusion is that relevant results can be used in business and investment decisions only if the impact of demographic transition on economic growth pattern is fully understood. Otherwise, it will be difficult to follow different investment suggestions based on the same concept of demographic dividends.

Slower economic growth with the disappearance of demographic dividends

In order to answer the questions of what the economic result will be as demographic dividends disappear, we should connect it with the dual-economy development theory. William Arthur Lewis, the 1979 recipient of the Nobel Prize in Economics, pointed out that a developing country's economy has the dual-sector economic structure with two contrasting sectors: a traditional agricultural sector and a modern industrial sector. The well-known dual economy development is a process where surplus labor in the agricultural sector is extracted and the Lewis turning point is approached when the growth rate of labor demand exceeds the growth rate of labor supply in the modern industrial sector at the existing wage rate. It should be clarified that the arrival of the turning point does not imply an absolute labor shortage, but instead means that labor demand can be fulfilled only if wages rise. The decreasing growth rate of the working-age population, which is caused by demographic transition, is the most important reason for leading unlimited labor supply to limited labor supply. Therefore, the disappearance of demographic dividends and the arrival of the Lewis turning point are inseparable. For example, China's annual growth rate of peasant workers' real wages is as high as 10.2%, when its annual increment of working-age population is decreasing at 13.6% in recent years.

Understanding the current changes in China based on development economics theory is not a pure academic argument. The main goal was to help us predict, a few years earlier, that since labor supply is no longer unlimited, (1) wages will inevitably rise, and this wage inflation will be accelerating; (2) the relationship of labor supply and labor demand will change dramatically; and (3) it is urgent to change the economic growth pattern. In any case, it is not a severe situation, in which we can only take caution after suffering a loss, even though economists denied the finding on the arrival of the Lewis turning point with careless doubt on the disappearance of demographic dividends.

Though always predicting the disappearance of demographic dividends and the arrival of the Lewis turning point, I am not the pessimistic Cassandra in the Greek mythology. In the light of the popular points of view in the academic and public fields, in what follows I will answer the following two questions: (1) will the comparative advantage in labor be lost as the Lewis turning point approaches?; and (2) will the economic growth rate be slower as demographic dividends disappear?

First of all, the comparative advantage and competitiveness in Chinese manufacturing industries will not be lost as wages rise with increasing labor productivity. The increase in average workers' wages is a significant reflection of the Lewis turning point in the labor market. The recent wage surge is simply a continuation of the rising wage rate trend since 2003. In fact, peasant workers' wages increased at 10.2% annually between 2003 and 2008. The wage rise satisfies the law of supply and demand in the labor market, which is affordable and welcomed.

The reason for this scenario arises from our relevant researches that conclude the growth of labor productivity does not only always accompany wage rise but also is faster than the wage raise in Chinese manufacturing industries. This gives the space for wages to rise faster over a period of time. It is also the only way to increase the proportion of labor remuneration in national income. The income raise of average workers and low-income families can substantially increase consumption and provide new driving force in demand for the economic growth.

At the same time, institutional improvement can not only extend to the traditional demographic dividends but also form the second demographic dividends. When explaining the phenomenon of "peasant worker shortage," some people believed that the household registration system and other institutional factors deterred labor transfer. I used to agree with this statement, but now I believe that changes in demographic structure play the fundamental role. However, institutional barriers indeed affect labor transfer, and demographic dividends are not fated, but can be maintained and extended if China can create the conditions.

Promoting the reform in household registration system, realizing the urbanization of peasant workers, and improving institutions that are in favor of increasing labor supply can exploit the potential of demographic dividends. Since the definition of the degree of urbanization in China is the proportion of resident population that reside in urban areas for six months or more, the degree of urbanization measured by the resident population was 45%, while the proportion measured by resident population with non-peasant household registration was only 33% in 2007. However, it is the institutional potential to exploit labor supply by eliminating the 12% difference so that peasant workers are no longer temporary residents, but permanent residents. In addition, it is a special opportunity window for China to keep its competitiveness by transferring labor-intensive manufacturing industries to the central and western areas and forming the domestic "flying-geese" model.

According to the main problems that need to be solved, China's economic growth can be divided into two future stages. In the first stage, the problem of "growing old before becoming rich" should be solved. It is not fearful to have an aging population, because, in fact, the degree of aging population is the highest in the richest countries. What China is facing is the relatively high degree of aging population with relatively low income per capita. For example, comparing China and other developing countries on the same development level, we will find that the degree of aging population in China exceeds that in any other country. However, if China becomes one of the high-income countries in the following 10 to 20 years, the degree of aging population in China will not be significantly high compare to other high-income countries. Therefore, it is key to maintain the rate of economic growth. All methods to exploit the first demographic dividends mentioned earlier are working to achieve this goal. After all, the problem of aging population is inevitable when economic growth approaches a certain level. As a result, we can only take precaution to look for the new engine for economic growth in the second stage.

Previously, I wrote a paper discussing the second demographic dividends. It proposed to use the changed demographic structure to create new institutional environment with aging population and eliminate the negative effect brought on by the disappearance of the first demographic dividends in order to exploit the source for sustainable economic growth in the long term. From the experiences of pioneer countries, these efforts should include: building up the retirement insurance system to accumulate capital in order to compensate the decreased saving rate with aging population; enhancing skill training and extending educational reforms to significantly improve the quality of human capital in order to accommodate the industry upgrading and the transition of economic growth pattern, as well as to break the bottleneck of labor shortage; developing and improving the labor market, forming appropriate labor relations; and eliminating the institutional barriers for increasing labor supply. We should have the following perception: the first demographic dividends will eventually deplete, but the potential of the second demographic dividends is unlimited.

Conclusion

As the originator of estimating its effects and predicting its future prospects, I am not superstitious to demographic dividends. In fact, more developed and richer countries are relying less on traditional demographic dividends to promote economic growth. To warn that demographic dividends are disappearing and the Lewis turning point has arrived in China is tantamount to appealing for the economic growth transitions to the productivity-driven pattern. The prediction of the East Asian miracle by the American economist Paul Krugman in his famous essay *The Myth of Asia's Miracle* became failure, because he did not realize that the assumption of diminishing marginal returns to capital could be violated with demographic dividends over a period of time, which means that the neo-classical economic growth theory was challenged in explaining the dual economy development in the developing economies' reality. However, the disappearance of demographic dividends implies that Krugman's economics is returning. That is, the source of sustainable economic growth will deplete without the increase of total factor productivity.

2.3. Extended Reading: Demographic Dividend: New Source of Economic Growth

Introduction

Since the 1990s, there has been an obvious breakthrough in the research on the relations between population change and economic growth. Before this, research on this domain was concentrated on the relations between the observation of population scale or the growth rate of population and the long-term economic growth achievements, and the conclusion was indefinite, namely there was evidence of both positive and negative relations.[1] However, after the central studies were transferred to the relations between the observation of population age structure and the economic growth achievements, it was discovered that the productive population structure, which the working-age populations had sustained growth, and the proportion enhanced unceasingly, which could provide an extra source for the economic growth or the demographic dividend through the sufficient labor supply and savings ratio enhancement guarantee. When explaining the "East Asian miracle" created by some countries and regions after the 1960s, such as Japan and the "Four Asian Tigers," as well as the aspect of the new continent economic growth historically surpassing the old continent economic growth in the West, some economists discovered that the improvement in population age structure had made a very large contribution to the drop in population dependency ratio, which might explain why it can exceed steady-state growth rate from 25% to 100% (Bloom and Williamson, 1997; Williamson, 1997).

Meanwhile, the existence of a demographic dividend in some countries and regions also responded to the mainstream economists' doubt of an "East Asian miracle." In neoclassic growth theory, it should be hypothesized that the progressive decrease in capital return is based on the shortage of labor. Therefore, if the improvement of the entire factor productivity target is not observed, any economic growth performance will be judged as unsustainable. For example, during the fast growth of the "Four Asian

---

[1] For example, the discussions on this aspect may be seen in Cai and Zhang *et al.* (2002, Chapter Two).

Tigers," Young (1992) and Krugman (1994) had doubted the so-called "East Asian miracle" because of the entire factor productivity performance of these economic bodies and concluded its growth would be unsustainable. However, in the economic development of infinite labor supply, before all surplus labors are admitted, the phenomenon of capital return decreasing progressively may not occur because of the existence of demographic dividend. That is, the condition of which other system environment can be guaranteed, it is sustainable for the growth way which mainly depends upon the growth of capital and labor investment in the process of dual-economy economic development. The validity of the growth type, which is different from the neoclassic growth theory, had been verified in East Asia's high-speed economic development (Williamson, 1997; Bhagwati, 1996). Obviously, the observation and explanation of demographic dividend are vitally significant in the economic growth theory.

The population factor played a similarly important role in China's high-speed economic growth during reform and opening-up, namely because the population policy, the economic growth, and the social vicissitude jointly impelled the population change during reform, the population structure presented the characteristics of many working-age populations, quick speed of increase, big proportion, etc., and formed an advantageous population structure, thus resulting in a latent demographic dividend. This dividend has realized the participation of economic globalization through the dual-economy development process on the premise that it created the system environment to conform to the market economy during reform and opening up (Cai, 2008). The research on economic growth indicated that, since the reform and opening-up policy, the economic growth rate may rise by 0.115 percentage points if China's gross dependency ratio lowers by 1 percentage point. From 1982 to 2000, the drop of the gross dependency ratio had impelled average GDP growth rate per person to rise 2.3 percentage points, which had contributed about one-fourth to average GDP growth per person in the same term (Cai and Wang, 2005).

Since the source of the demographic dividend is the age structure superiority produced at the specific stage of population change, this population age structure can change naturally along with the changes of population transformation stage; namely, it may change from the population structure of the working-age populations as the advantage to the aged population structure. In fact, the fast growth of working-age population of 15–64 year olds in the 1960s had entered a relatively slow growth in the 1990s, and it is estimated that it will stop growing around 2015. Meanwhile, the proportion of population of age 65 and above in all populations had approached 7% in 2000, and it is estimated that it will reach 9.6% in 2015. Correspondingly, a rise in the population dependency ratio will occur at that time.

If following the former definition about the demographic dividend (full labor supply and high savings ratio are guaranteed by the sustained growth of the working-age population and the unceasing enhancement of proportion), as well as the corresponding proxy variable of estimated demographic dividend (population dependency ratio), approaching to and arriving at the above turning point means the weakening, and even vanishing, of the demographic dividend. But, some literature also pointed out that, in the situation which the population structure continues to age, individual and family's precautions may have a new savings motive to form a new savings source, and its investments in domestic and international money market may also obtain the profits. This is called "the second demographic dividend," which differs from the demographic dividend in the fore-mentioned significance (Lee and Mason, 2006). However, if observed merely from a savings motive in the aging time, the second demographic dividend, which can be regarded in the same category with the first demographic dividend, still could not be formed in the impelling degree of economic growth action.

In understanding what causes the aging of a population, the fact that the population change from the initial phase of juvenile population decrease enters the phase of working-age population decrease in succession so that the proportion of aged populations in all populations is enhanced must be observed, however, the function of the enhancement of population life expectancy due to the life-span elongation is often neglected. We suppose that, even if the population age structure does not increase and decrease among the children group, the job-age group, and the elderly group, the aging degree observed according to this target the proportion of elderly in all populations defined will also increase if the elderly can live longer. Because of the economic and social development, the Chinese people's life expectancy rose from 67.8 years in 1982 to 73.0 years in 2005. Based on the condition of a healthy life-span elongation, the elderly will no longer be viewed as less-than precious human resources and human capital, therefore, the second demographic dividend can have a remarkable significance only in the observation from the labor supply and the human capital accumulation. This section discusses the second demographic dividend, which has identical significance with the first demographic dividend in reference to the labor supply and the savings ratio.

It is worth stressing that the use of demographic dividend is conditional, especially because it needs a series of system conditions. Numerous existing literatures indicated that, as for the developing countries, the key to overtaking developed countries is simply through faster growth than the developed countries, thus resulting in a convergence. But, this convergence is a conditional convergence, namely various latent factors of developing countries can become the practical source of economic growth by simply meeting a series of material and institutional conditions, thus a quicker economic growth can be realized (Sala-i-Martin, 1996). The drop of China's population dependency ratio started in the mid-1960s, but, only the reform and opening-up created the conditions to use the first demographic dividend. According to the definition, the second demographic dividend requires higher conditions, and it comes down to the reform of educational system, employment system, household registration system, and retirement security system.

Regarding the different countries, the first demographic dividend had different arrival times, therefore its departure times were different, even the obvious effects of demographic dividend cannot be discovered in many early developed countries. Therefore, along with the arrival of population aging, China does not actually have the problem of special population liabilities relative to other countries, although it has indeed enjoyed the contribution of demographic dividend to the economic growth. China only needs to avoid a "vacuum period" of demographic dividend between the acquisitions of first and second demographic dividend. If China continues this route, which extends the first demographic dividend while creating the conditions for second demographic dividend, it may avoid the negative influence brought by the aging of populations to the economic growth, and maintain sustained economic growth. This section will mainly discuss the conditions for the second demographic dividend, how to avoid the vacuum phenomenon between two demographic dividends, and how to lengthen the first demographic dividend.

Savings motive, savings source, and social security system

According to the general life cycle, a person belongs to the juvenile dependent population before reaching the working age and then becomes a member of the productive population through employment after reaching the working-age, and finally becomes a member of the elderly dependent population after withdrawing from the labor market. Correspondingly, the period of employment mainly concentrates on persons aged between 20 and 65 years, namely, the actual time of employment is postponed for ~4–5 years over the initial working age because the period for obtaining an education has expanded. On the other hand, irrespective of whether a person obtains labor income, his/her consumption actually occurs for the entire life. Thus, the life cycle characteristic of individual labor income and consumption is formed, namely the relatively invariable consumption is maintained for life, but the labor income only starts when a person is about 20 years old, is rapidly enhanced afterward, and is stable in the high level in the ages between ~25–45 years, and then drops gradually, until vanishing at about 65 years old (Figure 2.1).

Because of the incomplete corresponding nature during the period of labor income and consumption, the individual, family, and even society, must make provisions to balance relatively invariable consumption for life by non-uniform incomes during different periods. Therefore, according to the definition of first demographic dividend, the bigger the scale of the working-age population, and the higher the proportion in all populations, the stronger the latent savings ability, and the high savings ratio may occur on the premise that other conditions are invariable. However, if this logic is inferred and deducted, the savings ratio may drop when the growth rate of working-age populations slows; its absolute quantity may also drop, while the aging degree enhances. However, just like some analyses on the condition of aging, the savings motive, as well as preserving and increasing the value of the savings for the future, is still feasible, but the question

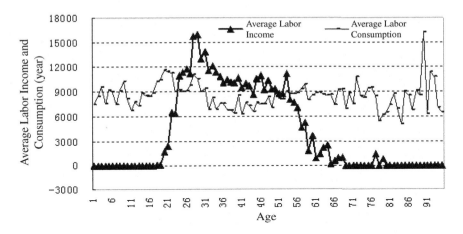

Figure 2.1. Life Cycle of Individual Labor Income and Consumption.

Source: Data from "Survey to urban labors in China" by the Institute of Population and Labor Economics, Chinese Academy of Social Sciences.

of whether it can be realized will be answered by the corresponding system conditions, especially by the nature of retirement security system (Lee and Mason, 2006). That is, its savings motive cannot be stimulated because the pay-as-you-go retirement security system causes future dependent populations to not to need to rely on own accumulation of retirement funds.

Since China implemented a double-support pattern, which unifies overall social planning of basic endowment insurance and individual account, two accounts implemented the mixed account management for the long-term; under this situation of large-scale historical debts, the individual account was used as the expenditure of overall planning funds to form the empty account. Until 2001, since the individual account reform was implemented in the Liaoning Province, the basic endowment insurance funds were accumulated to a certain extent, namely the balance between revenue and expenditure accumulated every year. This reform was further expanded to the Heilongjiang and Jilin Provinces, and then the experiment was carried out in eight other provinces, cities, and autonomous regions. Although the balance between revenue and expenditure of basic endowment insurance fund or the accumulation of individual account had expansion along with the increase of experimental provinces, the total accumulated level was very limited because the payment rate had gradually reduced, as well as because a majority of provinces had not yet implemented this reform. Until 2007, an individual account balance of about 11 trillion Yuan, only 7% were realized actually, namely the accumulated balance of more than 700 billion Yuan (Figure 2.2). Moreover, the distribution of this accumulated balance was highly concentrated; only six provinces (Guangdong, Zhejiang, Jiangsu, Shandong, Heilongjiang, and Liaoning) accounted for 51% of the country's accumulated balance of basic endowment insurance funds in 2006.

However, the "pay-as-you-go" system is unsustainable because it was established based on the availability of a large-scale working-age populations, high proportion, and low population dependency ratio, and requires a higher labor support productivity if the above conditions are changed. Generally, because of the enhancement in life expectancy and the drop in fertility rate, the proportion of dependent populations changes. Because of this, it is inevitable that the "pay-as-you-go" system will go through the following three adjustments, or some combination among the three, to solve the endowment insurance fund shortage problem: (1) enhance the level of tax revenue or compulsory payment; (2) reduce the pension

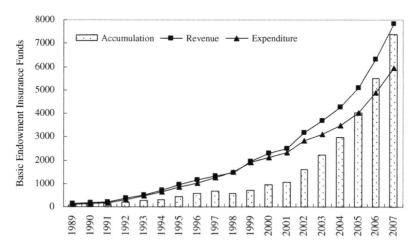

Figure 2.2. Revenue and Expenditure and the Accumulation of Basic Endowment Insurance Funds.

Source: Data from *"China Statistical Yearbook 2008"* of National Bureau of Statistics (国家统计局).

payment level; and (3) enhance the age requirements of pension drawing (Turner, 2006). However, the problem may be greatly alleviated if the individual account is accumulated early. A simulation study indicated that, if the current "pay-as-you-go" retirement security system is changed to a completely accumulated individual account system, a number of retirees may provide for the aged who are not completely dependent upon the "pay-as-you-go" system by 2020, thus the social retirement burden rate may be greatly reduced (Cai and Meng, 2004).

Life Expectancy, Retirement Age, and Labor Supply

As a result of population change, the aging of populations reflects not only the proportional changes among different age groups but also the enhancement of population life expectancy, namely the result of enhanced longevity. Jointly considering the factors of health and human capital accumulation (including education, training, and managing middle schools), the effective job age should be lengthened along with the enhancement of life expectancy. If this should occur, it would mean expanding working-age population scale and reducing the retired populations supported by every working-age population through the postponement of the actual retirement age. It is important to note that the legal retirement age is different from the actual retirement age, namely, under the situation which the legal retirement age has been established, there could be a large deviation in the actual retirement age because of the labor market condition. According to some survey findings, the actual retirement age of Chinese urban workers was 51 years in 2005, which was different from the legal retirement age of 60 years for men and 55 years for women adopted by the majority.

From Figure 2.3, we can discover that what can truly change the population years of service, thus changing the support ability for the elderly is the actual retirement age, but is not directly linked to the legal retirement age. If changes are only made to the legal retirement age, but the labor market is unable to fully admit these populations, it would mean that their choice of employment and retirement is revoked, and this population will have a serious fragile status. Figure 2.3 reveals that the effect of lengthening the actual retirement age from 50 to 60 years may reduce the

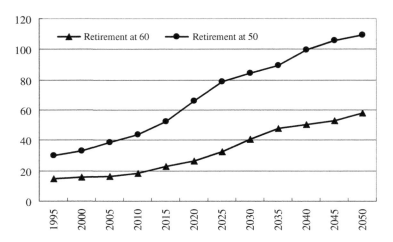

Figure 2.3.   Different Actual Retirement Age and Different Dependency Ratio.
Source: Data from United Nations (2003).

old population dependency ratio, namely older populations which need
support from working-age populations, are reduced from 109 to 58 in
2050. Although increasing the legal retirement age in developed countries
becomes the method for dealing with aging and is widely used because of
insufficient pension funds, this method should not become the choice
method in the near future because China's situation is entirely different
from that of the developed countries in two important conditions, which
will be explained in the following paragraphs.

First, there are different normal supply–demand relations in the labor
market. Labor shortage was a natural aspect of the development phase in
the majority of developed countries. In addition, the basic supposition of
economics takes the West as the example, but China did not actually form
the universal labor shortage normal although it was surmounting the phase
of infinite labor supply (Cai, 2008). It means that, in the West, the extension of legal retirement age may provide a stronger work motivation for
workers because the labor market needs a supplemental labor supply, but,
as for China, a similar policy actually means reducing the worker's choice
space, even though it is highly possible this will weaken the older workers. In turn, this will result in unemployment and an inability to obtain
their retirement pension for sometime.

Next, different worker groups have different life expectancies after retirement. The life expectancy is the comprehensive target that reflects the population health condition, which is influenced by the level of economic and social development in the aggregate level, and is closely associated with the income of different population groups, the medical service, and even the educational level of the individual. Therefore, different groups of a similar retirement age have different surplus life-spans after retirement, thus the time span for pension drawing varies. For example, even if in the U.S., where overall income and medical service levels were high, for the surplus life-span of populations aged 65 years in the 67-year-old group in 1997, women reached as high as 19.2 years while all populations reached 17.7 years, but, men in low-income group were only 11.3 years (Weller, 2000). The difference in life expectancy should be much more remarkable in China. From the disparity among regions, in 2000, life expectancy was 79.0 years in Shanghai, but only 65.5 years in Guizhou (Capital University of Economics and Business Task Group, 2007, p. 524). Although the life expectancy data of various age groups is incomplete, the retired populations' surplus life expectancy can have more differences because China has a greater income differential than the U.S.,[2] and the social security coverage is very low. A public policy is operable only if it contains a fair idea of its design in the beginning.

Third, the overall characteristics of labors, weighed by the human capital as the main standard, are different. At present, China's labor group, which approaches retirement, is the transitional and transformation generation. As a result of this history, their human capital talent would not place them at a competitive position in the labor market. The feasible premise is that an older worker's education level does not have a remarkable difference from that of the younger worker, with the addition of their work experiences, thus the older worker has a competitive power in the labor market. For example, in the U.S.'s working-age populations, the number of years of education in the 20-year-old population is 12.6 years, but the education years in the 60-year-old population is 13.7 years. At present, in China's working-age populations, the older the people, the

---

[2] For example, in 2000, the Gini coefficients of U.S. and China were 0.41 and 0.45, respectively (China Development Research Foundation (中国发展研究基金会), 2005, p. 13).

lower the educational level. For example, the number of years of education drop from 9 years at 20 years old to 6 years at 60 years old, but the
disparity, which is 29% lower than the U.S. at 20 years, has been expanded
to 56% lower at 60 years (Figure 2.4).

In this case, once the retirement age is extended, workers in the older
group will fall into an unfavorable competitive position. However, in
recent years, although the employment pressure has reduced, their competitive position has remained relatively unchanged. It was calculated,
according to the data of 1% of population sampling survey in 2005, that
the urban and rural working-age populations' work participation rate had
dropped to around 45 years. For example, the urban work participation
rate had reduced from 85.9% at 35–44 years to 69.3% at 45–54 years, and
then reduced to 23.1% at 55 years and above. But, the rural work participation rate reduced from 94.8% at 35–44 years to 90.7% at 45–54 years,
and then reduced to 51.9% at 55 years and above. For the urban workers,
the untimely drop in the work participation rate is not caused by voluntary
choice, but through the "depressed worker effect." Obviously, expanding
the overall labor scale and reducing the social dependency burden of the
elderly will not directly benefit those currently approaching retirement
age, but will create the ideal conditions for the current generation of

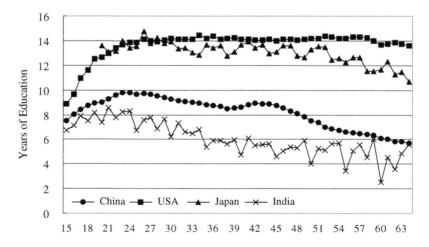

Figure 2.4.   Different Age Groups' International Educational Level.
Source: Data from Wang and Niu (2009).

young people when they reach retirement age. This will allow them to gradually develop into workers who have more sufficient human capitals, and who will have the ability to extend their years of service. Current labor resources can be fully used to lengthen the first demographic dividend and create the conditions for the arrival of second demographic dividend by maintaining the sustainable source of Chinese economic growth to create a strong labor demand. During the reform and opening up, the development of labor-intensive industry, which is mainly concentrated in the coastal areas and which adapts to China's comparative superiority, is the biggest creator of non-agricultural industrial posts. With the slowing of the working-age population growth speed, as well as the admittance of job enlargement to rural surplus labors, the characteristic of infinite labor supply is vanishing (Cai, 2008), and the coastal area has directly felt the pressure of labor cost rise. Because of the wide Chinese territory, there were huge differences between areas in the level of development and resource talent. In addition, the industrial transfer pattern between countries that occurred throughout world economics history, namely the so-called "Flying Geese Pattern" (see Kojima, 2000), may become the domestic industrial transfer path. Thus, through the transfer of the labor-intensive industry from the eastern area to the mid and western areas, the existing labors are fully used to lengthen the first demographic dividend.

Human Capital, Labor Productivity, and Comparative Advantage

Although the demographic dividend concept refers to the productive population structure and has positive influence of two economic growth conditions, the savings ratio and the labor supply, the human capital factor is actually contained in the labor supply. As mentioned earlier, in the process of the aging of populations, the scale of the working-age population may still be expanded through the arrangement of the labor market system, thus sufficient labor supplies would be maintained. In addition, on the premise of deepening education, the change of population age structure must have no negative influence on the accumulation of human capital. On the contrary, the change of population structure has also created some new, positive conditions, which would be advantageous to expanding and deepening education and may be regarded as the second demographic dividend of new economic growth source created from the human capital.

The changes in age structure caused by the population change are manifested through the percentage of the population who receive an elementary-level education (i.e., juveniles aged 5–14 years old) and the proportion in total populations to assume the falling tendency. What is relative to this falling tendency is moderately lagged track change of the working-age population, namely the latter presents the anticipated changes which first rise, then stabilize, and subsequently drop. The change in the relations of populations in these two age groups will unify into a falling tendency of the quantity, which working-age populations provide for school-age populations (Figure 2.5). The economic meaning of this phenomenon is as follows: the restriction to educational resources will have obvious alleviation along with the change of population structure, thus, the country, the family, and society may use more resources for the further expansion and deepening of education. As shown in Figure 2.5, under the situation which the ratio between school-age populations in the 5–14-year-old group and working-age populations in the 15–59-year-old age group (school-age populations' dependency ratio) goes down (See Scene I in Figure 2.5), the school age may be conditionally enhanced to the group at 5–19 years, and the ratio between this group and working-age populations in the 20–59-year-old age group will also drop simultaneously (See Scene II in Figure 2.5), thus serious resource restriction does not occur. Under the situation, which, at present, has a high diffusion rate of compulsory education, so does it. If the actual retirement age can be enhanced in the future again, the resource restriction will be reduced further.

During the 30-year reform and opening up, China's educational level has been greatly enhanced, and higher and vocational education have also seen considerable development, while compulsory education has been evenly spread. However, China's education development level continues to have a large disparity from developed countries, and between urban and rural areas. For example, the enrollment ratio of developed countries is generally maintained at 100% before age 18, compared with China's enrollment ratio, which begins to drop drastically at age 12. When observing the differences in educational level between urban and

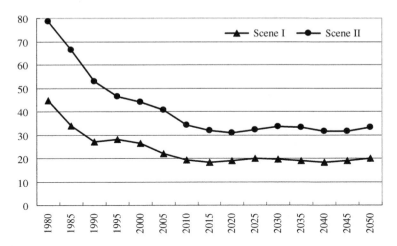

Figure 2.5. Working-Age Populations' Corresponding School-Age Populations.
Source: Data from United Nations (2003).
Note: 5–14 years as school age and 15–59 years as working age in Scene I; 5–19 years as school age and 15–59 years as working age in Scene II.

rural areas, a similar change track may also be seen. On one hand, this is no doubt about the restriction factor for the enhancement of labor productivity; on the other hand, it will also have a huge potential to meet an objective of enhancing labor productivity through the deepening of education for the future. Theories and experiences indicate that the overall improvement of the educational level is the main foundation for enhancing labor productivity. A quantitative analysis indicated that, in the manufacturing industry, labor productivity will rise 17% if the staff's education level is enhanced by one year. If the academic credentials of enterprise staff who have education up to junior middle school can be improved to the level of senior high school, the enterprise's labor productivity will be enhanced by 24%, and if they can be further improved to the level of junior college, the labor productivity may be enhanced by 66% (Qu, 2008).

Many judgments on the comparative superiority of China's labor-intensive products and international competitive power are biased in their observations. If observing purely from the wage level, the enhancement of labor cost means the weakening of comparative superiority. According to this knowledge, before the international financial crisis affected China' entity economy, the wage level rose quickly in recent years, along with the appearance of the labor shortage phenomenon, which undoubtedly has weakened the competitive advantage of the Chinese manufacturing industry. However, a national or local product's comparative advantage and competitive power are by no means completely decided by the wage level, and are also decided by the labor productivity level. Specifically speaking, it should be understood from the target of union wages and labor productivity, namely the ratio between relative wage level and relative labor productivity level ("unit labor cost advantage") (Ark, 2008). Even if the wage rate has begun to enhance, this target may be still maintained at low level so long as the labor productivity has a faster rate of enhancement, thus meaning that the industrial comparative advantage and the competitive power can still be maintained. But, this supposition was the reality of the Chinese manufacturing industry in 2000–2006, namely, the wages rose but the labor productivity had quicker enhancement: the annual mean rate of descent of "unit labor cost advantage" in eastern, middle, and western areas was 7.6%, 11.3%, and 8.3%, respectively (Qu, 2008). Under the situation in which the labor-intensive manufacturing industry gradually realizes the interregional transfer, the huge potential, which enhances the labor productivity through the deepening of education in mid and western areas, may cause the Chinese manufacturing industry to maintain their competitive advantage, thus to continue the demographic dividend.

Chapter 3

End of the Unlimited Labor Supply Era in China

3.1. The Era of Unlimited Labor Supply Ends in China

Introduction

Since the emergence of the "peasant worker shortage" in the Pearl River Delta area in 2004, labor shortage did not disappear or relieve, but spread to other regions in China, even the central and western regions where labor force used to be exported. There was even more severe shortage of the average worker in China in 2007. This phenomenon is not short-term or cyclical but has arisen from\ the changes in phases of demographic transition and economic growth, which implies that the Lewis turning point has arrived. Therefore, it is necessary to understand that the changes in the long-term relationship of labor supply and labor demand and its implication for sustainable economic growth has significant meaning for China's policy making and economy trend prediction.

A significant policy implication exists for a developing country to transition from having an unlimited labor supply to incurring labor shortage. However, no country actually reached the turning point in the years when Lewisian dual economy development theory was prevalent. Then, neo-classic economics theory became popular when Japan and the "Four Tigers" in Asia consecutively passed the Lewis turning point, and the international economics society did not conclude experiences and lessons from the view of the turning point. Therefore, China has no experience to follow when facing this phase change in economic growth. It is a challenge for China to develop its own explanations on economic development and macroeconomic growth, which also enables China to make great contribution to economics with its unique experiences. This chapter does not intend to answer these challenges, but primarily raise relevant questions and give preliminary discussions on the policy implications of arrival of the Lewis turning point.

Basic facts

Although the labor market situation is not determined by the aggregate quantity of labor, the characteristic transition from unlimited labor supply to labor shortage is the result of changes in aggregate quantity of labor, i.e., changes in demographic structure. China accomplished the demographic transition in a much shorter period of time than the developed countries previously did (i.e., it only took a little over 20 years to transition from high fertility rate to low fertility rate), therefore, the characteristic change from unlimited labor supply to labor shortage in the course of dual economy development arrives much earlier than in other countries because of both the unique demographic transition and unprecedented economic growth.

Taking into account the factors of urbanization, though the proportion of the working-age population aged between 15 and 64 years is still currently increasing, it is predicted that the proportion of the working-age population will first stop increasing in 2013, then start decreasing afterward. For example, the proportion of China's working-age population increased from 72.1% to 72.3% between 2005 and 2006 and was predicted to increase to 72.5% in 2007, but the proportion of working-age residents in urban areas started to decrease in 2005 and decreased from 76.2% in 2005 to 76.1% in 2006 and 76.0% in 2007. Therefore, the "peasant worker shortage" is not a short-term or cyclical phenomenon, but a phase change trend from unlimited labor supply to labor shortage because of the changes in demographic structure.

The labor force configuration in rural areas supports the finding on the arrival of the Lewis turning point. It is a conservative estimate that over 200 million in the 485 million rural labor forces migrated to non-agricultural industries by working locally or remotely in 2005, 178 million labor forces are still demanded in agriculture, and half of the remaining 100 million

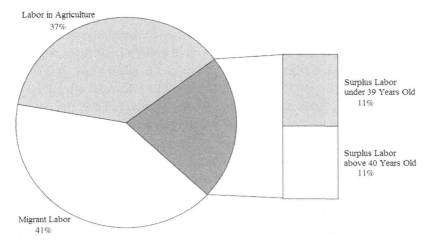

Figure 3.1. Labor Force Configuration in Rural Areas in 2005.

labor forces in the rural areas are above 40 years old (see Figure 3.1). This means that the widespread "peasant worker shortage" has arisen because the rural labor migration scale does not satisfy the demand of fast economic growth with the current incentive mechanism and incentive level.

According to the dual-sector economic growth theory, characteristics of the dual-sector economic structure will begin changing when the reservoir of rural surplus labor dwindles. This does not mean that there is no potential of migrating labor from rural areas, but implies that the non-agricultural industries cannot easily absorb labor supply as it is in the typical dual-sector economic growth period if wages do not rise or equivalent incentive mechanism is not enhanced. Based on this implication, we call the unprecedented phenomenon that is currently observed in China the "Lewis turning point."

Policy implications

The implication to sustainable economic growth

China's fast economic growth after the reform and opening-up benefits from demographic dividends brought on by the early-accomplished demographic transition. With sufficient labor supply and high savings rate, production inputs did not encounter diminishing marginal returns to capital, which is predicted in the neoclassical economic growth theory. Therefore, the input-driven economic growth pattern performed well for a long time in China. Earlier estimates show that the growth rate of GDP per capita will increase 0.115% as dependency ratio decreases by 1%, i.e., demographic dividends will contribute to the growth of GDP per capita at least 26.8%. However, this occurrence also reversely holds that the growth rate of GDP per capita will decrease 0.115% as dependency ratio increases 1%. It is predicted that the dependency ratio will start increasing after 2013 and demographic dividends will convert to demographic debt at that time. This implies the end of the unlimited labor supply era in China and calls for a transition from the input-driven economic growth pattern to the productivity-driven economic growth pattern (the essence of the economic growth pattern transition). Otherwise, the source of fast economic growth will disappear.

Implications to macro economy

With the widespread labor shortages, average workers' wages tend to rise. For example, a conservative data shows that peasant workers' wages increased 2.8% in 2004, 6.5% in 2005, and 11.5% in 2006.

Since wage raises caused by labor shortage have significant income effects for the widest range of middle- and low-income families, these families' high consumption tendency promotes slight inflation, which is mainly driven by the rising food prices.

If average workers' wages increase enough to expand labor participation and absorb sufficient labor supply for the needs of non-agricultural industries, then we will observe that labor shortage disappears or reduces. However, labor shortage is still widespread and has the tendency to become increasingly intense in recent years. This fact shows that the wage raise has not yet reached the labor market clearing level. With our estimates on the aggregate quantity of labor supply, it is predicted that labor shortage will not disappear in 2008, but the wages of average workers, especially of peasant workers, will continue to increase. Accordingly, because of the large proportion of food and clothing in retail sales, strong consumption demand for general commodities will form a slight cost-driven inflation pressure. Since the wage raise is supported by the continually increasing labor productivity, the stability of China's macro economy will not be harmed. According to estimates by the International Labor Organization, the growth rate of labor productivity in China was the fastest in the world between 1980 and 2005, with an annual growth rate of 5.7–7.9% in the manufacturing industries. However, considering that it is just the beginning of average workers' wage raise and the consumption ability of low-income families is still vulnerable, inflation may deter consumption growth and cause ups and downs in consumption when taking into account production fluctuations.

Implications to the world economy

China has made sufficient use of its demographic dividends to promote fast economic growth, which is reflected in China's labor-intensive manufacturing products, which have the comparative advantage and gain competitiveness in the global market, creating huge trade surplus. China has the revealed comparative advantage in international trade mainly because it has abundant and inexpensive labor and it is also a more realistic factor than the exchange rate for China to provide affordable products with superior quality to the residents of importing countries. Although the long-term relationship of labor supply and labor demand will transform into increased labor cost for enterprises caused by the average workers' wage increase and is already reflected in higher prices for the products made in China in the importing countries' markets, the wage rate in China is still much lower than that in the United States and other developed countries. In addition, China's trade partners have enough space to absorb this inflation pressure, so the competitiveness of the products made in China will not be harmed.

In the condition that labor cost has increased, the appreciation of RMB should be further slowed to avoid "pouring oil on the fire" for the comparative advantage of China's manufacturing products and oversuppressing the export growth rate. It will harm China's domestic employment and shock the consumption of low- and middle-income consumers abroad. Even in the condition that the exchange rate leverage is less used, we can predict that the problem of China's too-fast trade surplus growth can be relieved by 2008 or later.

Implications to institutional changes

The dual-sector economic structure is essentially a result of institutional settings; it creates the paradox that there is continual surplus labor supply in the rural areas, while the institutional factors deter the integration of rural and urban labor markets. For example, China's household registration system, which creates barriers for smooth labor migration between rural and urban areas, has caused severe fragmentation of the labor market. The end of the unlimited labor supply implies that the phase change in economic growth provides the condition upon which China can fundamentally transform the labor market fragmentation. In fact, an important new characteristic after the reform and opening-up is that the government can better adapt to the reality of institutional needs and provide more efficient institutional services.

Therefore, in 2008, we can have optimistic expectations of the government policy changes, especially the reforms. In the areas of public services, social security system, and the integration of rural and urban labor markets, greater efforts and more breakthroughs will be seen from the government, especially in the reforms of the household registration system, equal employment opportunity, and equal rights for public services.

3.2. The "Peasant Worker Shortage" Reflects the New Relationship of Labor Supply and Labor Demand

The "peasant worker shortage" became a nationwide labor shortage (including in labor exporting areas) around the spring festival in 2010. There are varying opinions surrounding this phenomenon. Generally speaking, media and audiences, scholars, and policy makers all had strong reactions and present their own views. However, the explanation of this phenomenon differs between each person and preference. Although there are common and complementary understandings in every aspect of the problem, we can also find the inconsistencies in these explanations, which may become confusing and difficult to follow.

The consistency of theories is important as we explain a phenomenon surrounding the reality of these theories. Although those scholars who used to be critical of my finding on the arrival of the Lewis turning point and the disappearance of demographic dividends have changed their minds and used my finding to explain the current "peasant worker shortage," their words reflect inconsistent information. In addition, their theories lack confidence when facing the statements that deny the fundamental changes in the labor supply and demand relationship because they did not logically connect the changes in the labor market in the past years or integrate their analysis in a consistent framework. Therefore, no correct policy suggestion can be provided to the policy makers.

We made a prediction on labor supply and labor demand a few years ago: if using the working-age population as labor supply and combining high, medium, and low GDP growth rates with high and low employment elasticities, six scenarios of labor demand exist. The prediction shows that the transition from labor supply exceeding labor demand to labor demand exceeding labor supply will occur between 2004 and 2009. It is interesting to observe that the start and the end of this time period were exactly the two years when the phenomenon of "peasant worker shortage" was highlighted, despite that the "peasant worker shortage" in 2009 was delayed after the spring festival due to the financial crisis.

However, I am reluctant to state that labor demand will exceed labor supply in the future, as I did not agree on the statement that labor supply had long exceeded labor demand in the past. When explaining the prediction results above, I explained to the media that economists sometimes make predictions, because they do not want to see the outcomes occurring at all. However, we should give additional explanations on the changeable variables and variables that were not expected to change in the prediction. In addition, we should point out the variables that were not included in the prediction.

In particular, the trend of the decline in working-age population, which is the base of labor supply, cannot be changed. In other words, the average annual growth rate of the population in this age group has decreased to just above 1% after 2002 and is predicted to become zero in 2013 and turn to a negative percentage upon the disappearance of conventional demographic dividends. This trend is the result of the population reproduction transition from "high birth rate, low mortality rate, and high natural growth rate" to "low birth rate, low mortality rate, and low natural growth rate." The demographic transition that occurs with economic growth and social development is irreversible and cannot be changed by adjustments on family planning policies. Economic growth, which determines labor demand, is not expected to be slower. My personal finding is that China's economic growth can continue its high pace in the following 10 to 20 years if the potential of the first demographic dividend can be released and the second demographic dividend can be exploited successfully. In fact, the mutable variable, which was not included in the prediction, is the wage rate. On one hand, the continual "peasant worker shortage" will lead to the increase of average workers' remuneration and achieve the expected arrival of the Kuznets turning point; on the other hand, along with the Lewis turning point, the wage rate can adjust the relationship of labor supply and labor demand and reduce the frequency of the "peasant worker shortage."

Therefore, neither the statement that labor supply exceeded labor demand in the past nor the assertion that there will be continual labor shortage can be the necessary condition for the government to determine the priority of employment problems and to make appropriate employment policies. In developed countries, labor is always the restrictive factor in economic growth, but most of the countries gave a higher priority to employment problems in their macroeconomic policy goals. In contrast, only by facing up to the changes in the labor market and the new characteristics of different worker groups' labor participation, can we effectively implement more proactive employment policies and macroeconomic policies according to their special needs in the labor market.

In the entire time period after the reform and opening-up, China has been in the double process of both the dual economy development and the institutional transition. In the labor market, three types of unemployment coexist with increases and declines. Macroeconomics and labor economics, which are based on the neoclassical economic theory, only deal with the cyclical unemployment, which is related to macroeconomic fluctuations, and the natural unemployment, which is affected by the frictional factors in labor market functions and the structural factors in technology improvements and industrial structure changes. With China's transition to the market economy, a larger amount of labor resources are deployed by the market mechanism and Chinese workers face the three types of unemployment mentioned above. In addition, as a dual-sector economy with the characteristic of unlimited labor supply, China also faces the problem of disguised unemployment, which is reflected as surplus rural labor and urban enterprise redundancy. An earlier estimate shows that surplus labor in rural and urban areas was 30–40% of the total labor population throughout 1980s and 1990s.

The labor market will experience fundamental changes after going through the following two separate processes. First, institutional barriers that deter labor migration are removed, a large amount of labor in rural areas migrate to the urban areas realizing remote non-agricultural employment, the level of surplus labor in agriculture is significantly reduced, and the age of half of the remaining labor in rural areas exceeds 40 years. The recent financial crisis shows that agriculture is no longer the reservoir of surplus labor, labor demand in urban areas is more rigid, and it is not possible for migrant labor from rural areas to return to agriculture. Second, with adjustments of the urban employment policy and reforms in which enterprises break the "iron rice bowl," the labor market is developing increasingly faster, labor in urban areas are eventually redeployed through market mechanisms, and the enterprise redundancy is absorbed to a large extent.

The redeployment mentioned above generally divides the worker groups in China's labor market according to their own characteristics and special employment difficulties. We can further observe from Figure 3.2 that the previous disguised unemployment is significantly reduced and it

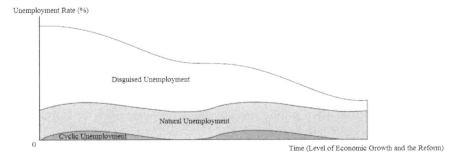

Figure 3.2. Types of Unemployment and Their Increases and Declines through In-depth Reforms.

is not the situation in which labor supply exceeds labor demand. However, there are various new characteristics for surplus rural labor and urban enterprise redundancy.

First of all, peasant workers become the main source of labor supply, though they are not well protected by labor market institutions. Most peasant workers are vulnerable to cyclical unemployment shocks, and they are either unemployed or in shortage with the changing macroeconomic climate. Through the urbanization of peasant workers and equalization of social security, proactive employment policies should reach this group to eliminate the institutional obstacles — namely, the existence of the household registration system, which prevent them from equal access to the public services in labor market.

Second, unemployed urban residents, who went through employment system reforms and labor market shocks at the turn of late 1990s and early 2000s, frequently face structural and frictional unemployment. Although they have achieved the employment pattern transformation through redeployment and realized reemployment from the status of redundancy-form disguised unemployment, a particular group of them with the fragility of human capital, and aged between 40 and 50 years old, are often caught in the dilemma of structural and frictional unemployment. For this particular worker group with employment difficulties, proactive employment policies should be more concerned about their capability of finding jobs and improving the implementation effects of social security policies.

Third, college graduates after enrollment expansion face mismatches between their job expectations and the demand in the labor market because of the specification of human capital. That is, the difficulties they encounter in the labor market are also of structural and frictional types. As the unemployed urban residents are eventually reemployed after experiencing the difficulties of being laid-off, the employment difficulty of college graduates, which is caused by enrollment expansion and mismatch of human capital, will exist in the long term. However, appropriate social protections and positive public employment services, such as trainings, can shorten this difficult process.

The changed labor market does not imply that proactive employment policies have accomplished their goals and the government's labor market policy orientation is still facing huge challenges. Analysis on the structural changes of different worker groups and their institutional needs provides helpful tools to understand the labor market structure and the employment situation and to define the role for promoting employment and labor market development. It also provides useful suggestions for assigning tasks among government departments, i.e., the macroeconomic regulation and control department should deal with the cyclical unemployment problem, the labor department should focus on the frictional unemployment problem and solve the structural unemployment problem together with the education department, and the social security department as well as the civil administration department should provide workers with sufficient social protections.

3.3. Maintaining Composure and Positively Responding to the Changes in Labor Relations

According to the definition given by the World Bank, China has stepped into the group of upper-middle income countries from the group of lower-middle income countries as its GDP per capita reached 3680 USD in 2009. From the experiences of many developing countries, members of society feel that fast income increases and acute social changes occur in this period and form higher expectations. If the expectations are consistent with the reality, then new senses of social identity are shaped and social harmony is enhanced. If the expectations are inconsistent with the reality, then a social identity crisis will occur, becoming a factor that harms the stability and cohesion of society.

With high-speed urbanization, labor mobility increases, and labor supply is no longer unlimited. At the new phase of development, people's dissatisfaction over land requisition compensation, income distribution inequality and wage growth below desired levels, slow improvement in working conditions, as well as unfairness of public services, will cause conflicts and oppositions on these matters. In fact, in China's transition from a middle-income country to a high-income country, the "growing pain" is inevitable, which calls for different policies from those used in the transition from a low-income country to a middle-income country.

Some developing countries have experienced this stage of development. Specifically, some Latin American countries did not accomplish the transition until now and even fell into the middle-income trap. Due to lack of awareness and findings on the changes of the development stage, Latin

American countries alternated between two policy tendencies. One is the populism policy, which involves making promises to the people beyond the nation's capability and usually results in empty promises. In the condition that did not hurt the vested interests, income differentials were increased, which caused more dissatisfaction from the people. The other tendency comes when the previous tendency does not work. In order to control the situation, these countries recentralized the power and even implemented the coercion policy, which resulted in further intense social contradictions and transferred the conflicts between workers and firms to the oppositions between the public and the government.

Changes in the relationship of labor supply and labor demand will definitely lead to adjustments in labor relations. Significant decrease in the growth rate of the working-age population, substantial reduction of surplus labor in agriculture, the widespread "peasant worker shortage," and average workers' wage increase all indicate the gradual disappearance of unlimited labor supply and the arrival of the Lewis turning point. It is an important turning point for the disappearance of the dual-sector economic structure and the inevitable stage through which a country moves from middle-income level to high-income level. Along with disappearance of the dual-sector economic structure are the dramatic changes in labor relations in that the workers will demand, to enhance the construction on the labor market institutions, and request the government to provide higher and equal social protection. We cannot avoid the situation because of the regularity of the phenomenon. The government should regard it positively and respond to the new situation with policy adjustments.

All previous successful experiences and failures show that the transition from a middle-income country to a high-income country will not proceed smoothly. It will be full of "growing pains," especially after reaching the Lewis turning point. China should adopt the correct policy to deal with this situation, overcome the middle-income trap, and, most importantly, make accurate judgments on the economic development stage and confront newly emerging problems and challenges. China must also fairly, transparently, and carefully guide public opinions and feelings, provide various forms of social psychological counseling, and enhance social cohesion.

First of all, the current new trend in labor relations is not an aggravated situation, but a predicted result of the changes in labor market. With a large amount of labor migration from the rural areas to the urban areas, the incomes of peasant workers are not fully reflected in the peasant household income statistics; the income differentials between urban and rural areas and its trend are overstated. Any policy-making in accordance with overestimation of rural–urban income gap based on insufficient empirical evidences would be unwise. It is the expression of higher expectations and the result of changes in the labor supply and demand relationship that new generations of peasant workers request higher incomes and better working conditions. When the Labor Dispute Arbitration Law reduces the costs of litigation suits on labor relations to zero, it further raises the average workers', especially peasant workers', enthusiasm, to protect their own rights. Therefore, the increase of labor dispute litigation cases does not imply that labor relations are aggravated.

Second, the function of the government is to promote the construction of labor market institutions. In the history of developed countries, when labor relations transitioned from that of conflict to relative harmony, it was not because the nature of labor opposition changed, rather, it was because the government built effective mechanisms to adjust labor relations through the construction of labor market institutions, including introducing labor legislations, establishing the minimum wages system, strengthening the role of unions, and forming the tri-party consultation mechanism, etc.

Third, the government should shift it focus from directly intervening in the economy to providing better public services and improving social protection mechanisms. The current stage of development provides the opportunity to form complete social protection mechanisms, i.e., use the government and society as the main body to develop an efficient labor market, reduce employment risks, improve residents' ability to secure their incomes and standards of living, and further reduce the incidences of poverty and vulnerability.

Social protection is a broader concept than development-orientated poverty relief, social insurance, social assistance, and social welfare. Relevant institutional arrangements include: (1) Developing employment policies and labor market institutions that are designed to protect the security of employment and rights of the workers; (2) Improving the social security system that is designed to protect residents from suffering unemployment, sickness, disability, and old age; and (3) Implementing social assistance to vulnerable groups with special difficulties, such as children, elderly people of "three-no" (no source of income, no ability to work, no supporters), and residents in specific areas, e.g., regions of exhaustion of resources.

In recent years, the United Nations' organizations, especially the United Nations Development Program, the World Bank, and the Asian Development Bank, are all advocating improving the social protection levels, and there are also a number of worthwhile results in academia. Establishing the social security system, developing the labor market, and innovating labor market institutions in this framework have become the action with consistent and complementary goals that will promote the improvement of human development and the reduction of social risks.

3.4. Extended Reading: Wage Increases, Wage Convergence, and the Lewis Turning Point in China

Abstract: We examine the wage trends of ordinary workers and the wage convergence between unskilled and skilled workers in China. First, we find that wages in all non-agricultural sectors, wages of migrant workers, and wages of hired workers in the agricultural sector have increased dramatically since 2003. Second, through comparing wage differentials between migrant and urban resident workers and between heterogeneous education groups within migrant workers, and by investigating the changes in the contribution of the returns to education to wage differentials, we find that the wages of unskilled and skilled workers have converged. Both the increasing wage trends and wage convergence are interpreted as evidence supporting the hypothesis that China has passed what can be called the Lewis turning point in the industrial sector. We conclude that the sustainability of economic growth in China requires an upgrading of labor market institutions to accommodate the merging of the rural and urban labor forces.

Introduction

In recent years, there have been an increasing number of empirical studies arguing whether or not the Chinese economy has met its Lewis turning point (e.g., Minami and Ma, 2010; Yao and Zhang, 2010; Zhang *et al.*, 2009; Cai, 2010a). The empirical evidence on this issue is mixed, and some important problems remain. First, clarifying the definition of the Lewis turning point would reconcile some earlier findings that seem to provide conflicting evidence. Second, analyzing the empirical results based on certain criteria regarding the Lewis turning point would help clarify the interpretation of those empirical results, which would also lead to a reconciliation of earlier results. In this study, we intend on providing more transparent evidence on the arrival of the Lewis turning point based on a clearer definition of it, and criteria that is largely agreed upon in the literature.

According to Lewis (1972) and Ranis and Fei (1961), the Lewis turning point can be referred to as the period during which expansion of labor demand exceeds that of labor supply and, as a result, the wage rate of ordinary workers starts to rise. At the same time, the wage rate in the agricultural sector is not yet determined by its marginal productivity of labor, and the difference of marginal productivities of labor between agricultural and non-agricultural sectors remains. In contrast, the commercial point refers to the time at which the wage rates in agricultural and non-agricultural sectors are both determined by their marginal productivities of labor, and the gap in productivities disappears. Only at this time does the dual economy end. However, in this study we focus on the Lewis turning point by examining wage trends.

Based on Japan's experience with the Lewis turning point, Minami (2010) suggests five characteristics of wage-related changes as criteria to test the arrival of the Lewis turning point. We have narrowed this list to two criteria: if the Lewis turning point arrives, one can empirically observe that (1) the wage rate in the subsistence sector becomes equal to the marginal product of labor and may show a bend from a constant (or slowly increasing trend) to a rapidly increasing trend; and (2) wage gaps between unskilled and skilled workers tend to close.

In a dual economy characterized by an unlimited supply of labor, the wage rate of ordinary workers typically remains constant at a subsistence level, above the marginal productivity of labor in agriculture. The reallocation of the agricultural surplus of labor to non-agricultural sectors in China began with the introduction of the household responsibility system in the farming sector and has made extraordinary progress as the institutional barriers deterring labor mobility were eliminated in the urban labor market. In the entire 30 years of the reform period, rural surplus labor has shifted from agricultural to rural non-agricultural sectors, and a mass migration ensued from rural to urban sectors and from central and western regions to coastal regions. Since labor policies have become more tolerant toward labor mobility across regions and sectors, migrant workers have become a significant component of employees and residents in urban areas. In 2009, the stock of rural laborers who migrated beyond township boundaries amounted to 145 million, which significantly mitigates the extent of labor surplus in the agricultural sector. Meanwhile, China's demographic transition has reached the point at which the increase in the working-age population is diminishing. Given the continuously increasing demand for labor, the growth of labor demand exceeds the growth of labor supply.

As a result, a labor shortage, composed of mainly migrant workers, resulted in the coastal areas in 2003, and subsequently became widespread throughout the country. As can be expected by theory, the wages of migrant workers substantially increased with an annual growth rate of 10.2% from 2003 to 2009. In addition, the wage rates of hired workers in agricultural sectors have also increased, indicating a decline of surplus labor in the agricultural sector, and a shortage of unskilled workers in urban areas, which has caused wages to rise in all sectors (Wang, 2010d). According to Lewis (1954), these phenomena indicate the advent of the Lewis turning point in the Chinese economy (Cai and Wang, 2010). This section provides an examination of the changing wage trends as a test of the Lewis turning point, and discusses their implications for the economic growth of China in the near future.

In the reform period, wage differentials among workers in China's labor market have been brought about by two factors. First, they are caused by differences in the returns to human capital, which reflects heterogeneity in educational attainment and skills of workers. Studies show that as the labor market develops, the returns to human capital tends to increase, which leads to larger wage differentials, and the contribution of heterogeneity in human capital to this increase also becomes more important (e.g., Zhang *et al.*, 2005). Second, they are caused by the discrimination against migrant workers and female workers. However, the contribution of this factor to wage differentials has fallen over time as the labor market matures (Wang and Cai, 2008; Wang, 2007).

In addition to the labor market maturation process, the changing relationship between demand for and supply of labor also tends to weaken the contributions of the above factors to wage differentials. In the pre-Lewis turning point period, there was an abundance of unskilled laborers and a scarcity of skilled workers. Therefore, as the labor market matured, only skilled workers were the bottleneck of workforce recruitment, and the wage gap between unskilled and skilled increased. Furthermore, not constrained by a labor shortage in general, employers tended to pay migrant workers at a wage rate lower than their marginal contribution to production by taking advantage of previously existing discriminatory institutions against workers without urban *hukou* (Knight and Song, 2005, p. 108). While the institutional ingredients discriminating against migrant workers have gradually disappeared as the reforms of employment policy and *hukou* policy have been implemented, wage discrimination against migrant workers persisted under the condition of unlimited supply of labor.

As the Lewis turning point is reached, the relative contribution of the changing relationship between demand for and supply of labor to the decline in wage differentials begins to dominate, which leads to wage convergence even if the factors causing wage differentials still exist. In addition, as the labor shortage becomes a constraint to enterprises' production, and causes substitution of physical capital for labor in agriculture, the marginal productivity of labor begins to play a role in determining wages. After the arrival of the Lewis turning point, new labor market conditions should induce changes in wage rates and wage differentials.

The Increasing Trend of Ordinary Workers' Wages

China's dual economy began in the early 1980s, a period in which the economic reform started and began to spur fast economic growth. The Chinese dual economy ended in 2003, which we refer to as a representative year of the Lewis turning point since a host of changes occurred in 2003, characterizing the turning point. The emergence of a dual economy in China was also accompanied by a transition from a planned economy to a market economy, and China inherited the legacy cost of the planned employment system. That is, during that period, the Chinese economy was characterized not only by its abundant laborers in agriculture but also by overstaffing in urban enterprises, which later led to massive layoffs and unemployment in urban areas. Therefore, the oversupply of labor was a normal condition at the time.

In the course of rapid economic growth, which has also been accompanied by fast social transformation, institutional obstacles deterring labor mobility between rural and urban sectors was gradually removed, and labor migration brought about a significant decline in the agricultural share of total employment. In the meantime, the reform of employment policy and the development of an urban labor market put an end to over-staffing in urban enterprises and reallocated the laid off and unemployed through a more competitive labor market mechanism.

In the same period, China experienced a radical demographic transition. As a result, total fertility dropped to below replacement level in the 1990s and the natural population growth rate decreased to 0.5% in 2009. Similar to what has occurred in many industrialized economies in their comparable phases, a demographic transition can lead to a changing pattern in labor supply. In particular, the growth of the working-age population accelerates at first, then grows at a decreasing rate, and finally stops growing in the end. China's working-age population is predicted to grow at a decreasing rate until 2013, at which time it will stop growing and shrink thereafter. All of these changes on the labor supply side indicate an end of unlimited supply of labor, which characterizes the dual economy.

On the other hand, the fast economic growth and resulting expansion of employment created a strong demand for labor. Together, the demographic and economic trends have changed the relationship between supply of and demand for labor. If we consider an annual increase of the working-age population between ages 16 and 64 years as labor supply and an annual increase of urban employment as labor demand, a comparison between the two trends can clearly show the changed situation of the labor market (Table 3.1). Since the number of laborers engaged in agriculture is in a declining trend, the non-agricultural sectors in rural areas are not expected to expand, and the increase of urban employees (including migrant workers) can adequately represent the overall demand for labor in the Chinese economy.

By combining various sources of employment data, we find that in 2009, 12.5% or 39 million of the 310 million urban employees were migrant workers. That is, urban employment statistics do not adequately account for the migrant workers. In fact, the total amount of migrant workers, who are defined as out-migrating from their home townships for more than six months, amounted to 145 million in 2009, of which 95.6% migrated to cities. We then compare the annual growth of the working-age population to the annual growth of urban employment, where the annual growth of urban employment is equal to the summation of increases in urban resident employees and migrant workers. As shown in Table 3.1, the phenomenon of labor supply exceeding labor demand can no longer characterize the Chinese labor market after 2003.

A related change is that the average age of the working-age population in rural areas is increasing as the population ages. Because labor migration from rural to urban sectors face not only physical and psychological costs, but also institutional barriers, older laborers in rural areas whose human capital endowment is relatively weak tend to be less capable of and

Table 3.1. Increment in Demand for and Supply of Labor Force (Million).

	Migrant workers	Urban resident workers	Working-age population
2003	9.20	4.78	13.58
2004	4.33	4.34	8.48
2005	7.55	4.27	11.49
2006	6.34	5.17	11.23
2007	4.85	5.45	10.08
2008	3.44	3.56	6.85
2009	4.92	3.76	8.46

Source: Authors' own calculation based on *China Statistical Yearbook* (various years), *China Yearbook of Rural Household Survey* (various years), and *China Population Yearbook* (various years).

less willing to migrate than their younger counterparts (Du and Wang, 2010). As a result, the actual supply of labor in rural areas is falling, and since there is an unremitting demand for labor in urban sectors, this causes a shortage of migrant workers.

The fast-growing increase in the wages of ordinary workers is indicative of such changes in the relationship between labor supply and demand, characterizing the current conditions of the labor market, and confirming the arrival of the Lewis turning point in China. To illustrate the new trend of unskilled workers' wages, we will present three selected categories of wage data. Instead of using aggregate data on the urban sector presented in statistical yearbooks, we use data on wages in the sectors employing mainly unskilled and semi-skilled workers, wages of migrant workers, and wages of agricultural workers. The reason for this is twofold. First, the urban employees, particularly in the state sector, are more or less protected in terms of wage determination (Knight and Song, 2005, p. 108), and data on wages in these formal sectors are too aggregated, thus the wage movement in these sectors is less representative for unskilled workers. Second, regular statistics on wages often omit wages of informal urban workers and migrant workers, so there is a need to seek out the wages of migrant workers to proxy for the wages of unskilled workers.

Various officially conducted surveys show that not only have the wages in manufacturing and construction increased, which mainly reflects the general trend of wages since they do not specifically represent the wages of migrant workers, migrant workers' wages in real terms have been catching up (Table 3.2). A new survey conducted by the National Bureau of Statistics (NBS) shows that real monthly wages of migrant workers amounted to 1221 Yuan in 2009, 90% higher than in 2001.

There exists some disagreement regarding the issues of whether there has been a significant increase in the wages of migrant workers and the causes of this increase. However, there are few studies that present evidence to support the opinions that either assert there is no significant increase, or that other factors rather than changing labor supply and demand conditions cause the increase in wages. Next, we weigh in on the debate by offering relatively general arguments.

First, we respond to the proposition that the growth in the wages of migrant workers is insignificant. Apart from the NBS source used in

Table 3.2. Real Wages and their Growth Rates by Sector (Yuan, %).

	Farm workers (daily wages)			Non-agricultural sectors (monthly wages)		
	Grains	**Pig farm**	**Cotton**	**Manuf.**	**Constr.**	**Migrants**
1998	18.43	9.60	19.70	589	621	
1999	14.26	9.64	11.83	658	674	
2000	19.00	10.13	19.72	733	732	
2001	18.25	10.49	18.35	813	789	643
2002	18.32	11.06	17.71	924	864	664
2003	18.73	11.21	18.43	1041	956	701
2004	21.40	18.63	25.81	1131	1029	755
2005	24.04	18.88	27.14	1250	1138	820
2006	27.73	22.36	27.77	1404	1282	887
2007	30.95	26.58	30.30	1562	1403	951
2008	37.85	29.52	32.09	1714	1525	1138
Annual growth rate	15.1	21.4	11.7	10.5	9.8	10.2

Source: Daily wages of grains, cotton, and pig farm worker with a size of over 50 are from Compilation of National Farm Product Cost-benefit Data; Monthly wages of manufacturing and construction are from China Labor Statistics (various years); Monthly wages of migrant workers are from NBS Statistical Report (various years).

Table 3.2, there are other surveys that show even higher levels and faster growth of migrant workers wages. For example, a 2010 survey conducted by the People's Bank of China shows that the average wage of migrant workers was 1783.2 Yuan in 2009, a 17.8% increase compared to the previous year (DSS-PBC, 2010, p. 40).

In fact, a comparison of the wages of local and migrant workers requires combining wage rates with working hours, because they do not work the same number of hours per week. According to a survey conducted in 2010 (called China Urban Labor Survey or CULS), migrant workers work 27% more hours a week than do urban local workers. That is, migrants must work for more hours per week in order to earn higher monthly wages. As a matter of fact, the same survey shows that while the wages of migrant workers were only 88.2% of the wages of local urban workers, the monthly wages of the former were slightly higher than that of the latter (5.6% higher) after adjusting for the difference in weekly working hours. That is, the growth of migrant workers' wages and their convergence to local urban workers' wages shown in Table 3.2 can imply a larger increase in the actual wage rate (e.g., if measured by the hourly wage rate).

Second, we respond to the propositions asserting that the scarcity of migrant workers is caused by other factors, such as the existing *hukou* system or higher educational attainment of the new generation of migrants, rather than by the changed relationship between labor demand and labor supply. The institutional barriers deterring labor mobility have been present throughout the planned and reform periods. In fact, the policies restricting labor mobility have been reformed rather rapidly and intensely in recent years, particularly since 2003 (see Cai, 2010e). While it is true that the new generation of migrants have higher educational attainment than previous generations, the educational attainment of migrant workers has improved over time, not just since 2003. Instead of its contribution to the increase in wages, we find that the contribution of education to wage differentials has declined in recent years, as is discussed in the next section. To strengthen the argument that it is the change in labor demand and supply that causes the increase in wages, we post the figures of the rapidly growing wages of workers in selected agricultural sectors in Table 3.2.

Wages Convergence in Labor Market

The wages of ordinary workers are, in essence, determined differently in pre- and post-Lewis turning point periods. Under the dual economy, the nature of unlimited labor supply was such that the marginal product of labor does not determine the wage rate for migrant workers moving from agricultural to non-agricultural sectors in urban areas. When passing through the Lewis turning point, the changing labor supply and demand conditions start affecting the wages for various groups, i.e., a relatively unchanged scarcity for skilled workers and increasing scarcity for unskilled workers. The determinant for the wage rate of migrants begins to shift from subsistence wages to marginal productivity of labor. Hence, wage convergence is expected to take place during such a peculiar period of time.

In the case of the Chinese labor market, as the Lewis turning point arrives, it is expected that wages converge between skilled and unskilled workers, between migrants and local residents, and across regions. By making use of the data from three waves of the CULS, we found an overall trend of wage convergence in the urban labor market. Pooling together both urban resident workers and migrant workers in urban areas, the calculated Gini coefficient of urban wages was 0.37 in 2001 and fell to 0.33 in 2010. The Calculated Theil Entropy index also fell from 0.25 to 0.19 in the same period. The existing wage inequality measured by other indices declined as well. The rest of this section discusses the wage convergence by groups of workers.

Wage convergence among migrant workers

Although migrant workers as a whole represent unskilled workers, there exists variation among migrant workers in terms of human capital. For example, among the 145 million migrant workers in 2009, 11.7% are primary schooled or illiterate, 64.8% finished junior high school, 13.1% finished senior high school, and 10.4% graduated from technical secondary school or above (DRS-NBS, 2010, p. 5). In other words, three-fourths of migrant workers are unskilled workers with whose maximum education level was a junior high school diploma. Migrants would not catch up with

Table 3.3.   Relative Returns to Education for Migrant Workers.

	CULS2001	CULS2005	CULS2010
Prim. School and below	−0.116 (0.039)	−0.119 (0.287)	−0.093 (0.032)
Sen. High School	**0.259 (0.040)***	**0.173 (0.030) ***	**0.169 (0.024) ***
Above Sen. High	**0.804 (0.084) ***	**0.753 (0.085) ***	**0.571(0.041) ***
Gender (male =1)	0.179 (0.031)	0.204 (0.022)	0.23 (0.019)
Experience	0.039 (0.044)	−0.0039 (0.0012)	0.022 (0.0029)
Squared experience	−0.00078 (0.0001)	−4.85e-07(1.48e-07)	−0.00058 (0.00006)
City dummies	Yes	Yes	Yes
No. of Obs	2283	3263	3499
Adj-R^2	0.197	0.162	0.238

Note: Standard errors are in parentheses, and *** means that the coefficient is significant at the 1% level.

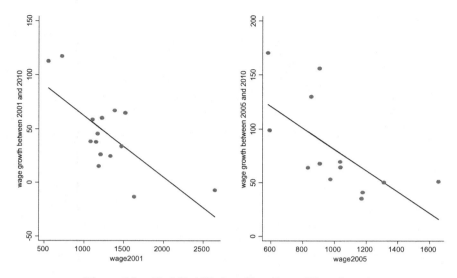

Figure 3.3. Unskilled Workers Have Faster Wage Growth.
Source: Authors' calculation from CULS data.

local workers' wage rates unless those unskilled workers have faster wage growth. Analysis from CULS data indicates that the Gini coefficient for migrant workers alone has decreased, from 0.396 in 2001 to 0.334 in 2005 and 0.319 in 2010.

Migrants' wage growth by education group is observed in Figure 3.3, where each dot represents real wage growth for a group of workers with the same educational attainment, the horizontal axis is the wage level in the base year (2001 and 2005, respectively) and the vertical axis is the wage growth from the base year to 2010. Although workers with higher educational attainment earn higher wages in all three rounds of the survey, Figure 3.3 clearly displays a circumstance in which workers with less education and lower wages in base years have a faster wage growth during the subsequent period.

To further understand the wage convergence within migrant workers and the driving forces of wage growth for unskilled workers, using CULS data, we investigate the return to education for skilled migrant workers relative to unskilled migrant workers. The estimation explains why the unskilled workers experience faster wage growth after the Lewis turning point, which narrows the gap of the returns to education between skilled and unskilled migrant workers. A typical Mincer regression is applied and the equation estimated is as follows:

The left-hand side variables are log earnings and explanatory variables that include the levels of last education (categorized by primary school or below, senior high school, and above senior high school), labor market experience and its square, gender, and city models.

As noted earlier, migrant workers who finished junior high school dominate the labor market, so this group is taken as the reference group. In Table 3.3, the regression results show that the relative returns to education for workers with above a senior high school education dropped from 80.4% in 2001 to 75.3% in 2005 and 57.1% in 2010, and that the relative returns to education for workers who just finished senior high school dropped from 25.9% in 2001 to 17.3% in 2005 and 16.9% in 2010. The declining trends of relative returns to education indicate that as the unlimited supply of labor ceases to exist, the marginal productivity of labor starts playing role in the wage formation of unskilled workers, whose lower educational attainment commands relatively higher returns in the labor market.

Wage convergence between local and migrant workers

Prior to the arrival of the Lewis turning point, a surplus of rural labor is the fundamental constraint that prevents the wages of migrant workers from increasing. In the meantime, the institutional segmentation in the urban labor market impedes migrant workers' access to work in formal sectors. Therefore, the institutional segmentation of migrant and local workers entails two different mechanisms of wage determination. On one hand, the unlimited supply of labor suppressed increases in the wages of migrant workers. On the other hand, the labor market segmentation protected local workers and discriminated against migrant workers.

After the Lewis turning point has been reached, a substantial change in the relationship between supply of and demand for migrant workers occurs. That is, the shortage of unskilled workers generates an upward pressure on the wages of migrant workers, who are at the low end of the wage distribution. Meanwhile, the institutionally determined wage is

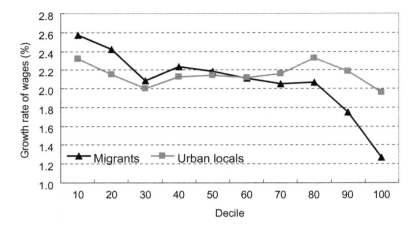

Figure 3.4.   Wage Growth Rates by Decile of 2001 (2001–2010).
Source: Authors' calculation from CULS data.

quickly eliminated. These two factors drive the wages of migrant workers upward and thus the wages of local and migrant workers converge.

Figure 3.4 shows the wage growth rates at each decile of the wage distribution in 2001 for both migrant workers and local workers during the period of 2001 to 2010. The figure shows that local workers had a relatively more stable wage growth across deciles, whereas migrant workers had greater variation of wage growth across deciles. First, migrant workers at the bottom of wage distribution in 2001 experienced faster wage growth than migrant workers at the top of wage distribution. Second, migrant workers at the bottom of wage distribution in 2001 tended to have faster wage growth than local workers at the same deciles in subsequent years, as evidenced by the migrant workers having higher growth rates at the six lowest deciles. These trends indicate that, with the gradual removal of the institutional barriers in the labor market, competitive forces were a major mechanism in the determination of wages.

To further examine the underlying reasons for the wage convergence between migrant workers and local workers, we pool together samples of both migrants and local workers to analyze the change in the role that the *hukou* identity plays in wage determination over time, while controlling for individual characteristics and localities of labor markets (city dummies). The estimation results (Table 3.4) show a diminishing effect of the *hukou* identity on wage determination. When controlling for other

Table 3.4. *Hukou's* Role in Wage Determination.

	CULS2001	CULS2005	CULS2010
Residence (migrants = 1)	**–0.107 (3.85) ***	**–0.087 (2.95) ***	**–0.048 (2.38) **
Years of schooling	0.102 (25.21)	0.098 (20.60)	0.11 (30.98)
Work experience	0.005 (1.89)	–0.001 (1.09)	0.018(6.48)
Squared experience	–0.0 (–1.20)	–0.0 (1.12)	–0.0 (–5.13)
Gender (male =1)	0.21 (10.50)	0.24 (11.07)	0.18 (11.05)
City dummies	Yes	Yes	Yes
Number of obs.	6260	6535	7940
Adj-R²	0.31	0.42	0.37

Note: *t*-statistics in parenthesis, *** significant at 1%, ** significant at 5%.

variables, the urban residence model variable explains 11% of the wage difference in 2001, 9% in 2005 and 5% in 2010. Considering that the magnitude of migration flow has been increasing and the total number of migrant workers in 2009 was 1.73 times as much as it was in 2001, the wage convergence between local and migrant workers will bridge the overall wage gaps in the labor market.

Wage convergence across regions

As the wages of migrant and local workers converge, and the labor market barriers are gradually eliminated, more adequate and integrated labor mobility across regions is expected to bring about a reduction of regional wage differentials. A previous study (Cai *et al.*, 2007) finds a convergence of migrant workers' wages across destination places after controlling for individual characteristics and the characteristics of sending areas. Following the same methodology, namely, by decomposing a suitable inequality index based on a wage regression, while controlling for individual characteristics and status of *hukou*, we can explore the contribution of regional factors to wage differentials.

Compared to conventional decomposition techniques, the regression-based decomposition is of merit (Fields, 1998, Bourgignon *et al.*, 1998, Morduch and Sicular, 2002). First, it allows us to avoid endogeneity that often appears when arranging inequality decomposition by category. In addition, it also makes it possible to look into the sources of inequality from continuous variables. Based on the estimation results from Table 3.4, we may decompose the wage inequality of migrants and local workers.

Following Shorrocks (1982), the inequality index may be written as a summation weighted by wage:

$$I(\mathbf{y}) = \sum a_i(\mathbf{y})y_i, \tag{1}$$

where $I(\mathbf{y})$ is the overall inequality index (e.g., the Theil entropy, Gini coefficient, or coefficient of variation), y_i is the wage for worker i, and $a_i(\mathbf{y})$ is the weight applied to each individual, which varies across different inequality indicators. Each regressor in the regression contributes to the inequality index. The share in overall inequality from factor k (explanatory variable or residual) is S^k, which is expressed as:

$$s^k = \frac{\sum_{i=1}^{n} a_i(\mathbf{y})y_i^k}{I(\mathbf{y})}. \tag{2}$$

Since it is determined by the regression coefficient $\hat{\beta}_k$ and the level of the factor x_k^i, the regression-based decomposition may be expressed as:

$$s^k = \hat{\beta}_k \left(\frac{\sum_{i=1}^{n} a_i(\mathbf{y})x_i^k}{I(\mathbf{y})} \right). \tag{3}$$

Regarding the inequality index used in this paper, Theil entropy, the index may be decomposed as:

$$I_{TT}(\mathbf{y}) = \frac{1}{n}\sum_{i=1}^{n} \frac{y_i}{\mu} \ln\left(\frac{y_i}{\mu}\right) \tag{4}$$

and

$$s_{TT}^k = \frac{\frac{1}{n}\sum_{i=1}^{n} y_i^k \ln\left(\frac{y_i}{\mu}\right)}{\frac{1}{n}\sum_{i=1}^{n} y_i \ln\left(\frac{y_i}{\mu}\right)}. \tag{5}$$

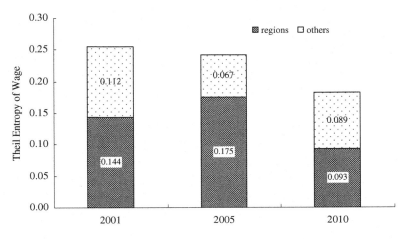

Figure 3.5. The Contribution of Regional Factors to Wage Inequality.
Source: Authors' calculation from CULS data.

Hence, according to the estimation results in Table 3.4, we compose the Theil entropy of wages by source of inequality and display the share from regional factors in Figure 3.5. The contribution of regional factors to inequality increased from 0.144 in 2001 to 0.175 in 2005, whereas it declined to 0.093 in 2010, and it was significantly lower than it was in 2001. In addition, the portion of regional factors that explains wage inequality declined from 56% in 2001 to 51% in 2010.

Conclusions and Policy Implications

The emergence of China's dual economy has been accelerated by a demographic transition that slows the increase of labor supply and by the fast growth of the economy that sustains the strong demand for labor. This reveals the changed relationship between labor demand and labor supply and its resulting upward pressure on wages that match the characteristics of the Lewis turning point. Whether this upward wage pressure is in fact a Lewis turning point or not, no one would deny that labor markets have become "tight" in many sectors and regions. Although pockets of "surplus" labor remain, China's economic growth begins to move towards a pattern framed by the neoclassical theory of growth. That is, further growth can only be sustained by augmenting total factor productivity (TFP), not by simply increasing inputs of physical capital and labor. Moreover, since the wage convergence between unskilled and skilled workers is one of the important features of the Lewis turning point, namely, low-income groups tend to benefit more from the general trend of increasing wages, the conditions of the Kuznets turning point, at which time income inequality first stops increasing and then begins falling, tends to emerge. A more balanced income distribution, however, is not spontaneous, but dependent on the effective functioning of labor market institutions and social protection mechanisms. The most fascinating outcome of the Lewis turning point is that, as income increases, the migrant workers contribute greatly to overall consumption, and thus contribute to the sustainability of its further growth. Next, we illustrate three challenges facing China due to the arrival of the Lewis turning point.

Shifting the economic growth mode

The neoclassical theory of growth assumes a diminishing return on capital because of the scarcity of labor. That is, without TFP growth, economic growth cannot be sustained by only adding inputs into the production process. When Krugman (1994), Young (1992), and other researchers criticized the "East Asian miracle," they did not take into account the unique feature of those economies at the time, namely an unlimited supply of labor. Thus, based on the neoclassical assumption, they mistakenly foretold an unsustainable future for the growth of those economies. As the Chinese economy gradually moves away from a scenario of unlimited supply of labor, however, those skeptical arguments have implications for China and for its sustainability of economic growth.

In their prominent study on the lost decade of the Japanese economy, Hayashi and Prescott (2002) suggest that it was the slow growth of productivity that caused the economy's stagnation. In 1990, when the population window was closed in Japan, it was already one of the richest countries in the world. However, in 2013, when the demographic dividend ends, China will have to come up against "aging before affluence." China should do everything in its power to transition into a more TFP-driven economic growth policy. Next, we illustrate two of the major challenges facing China to raise its productivity in manufacturing.

First, China's development strategy to defy comparative advantage tends to harm the resource reallocation effects potentially to be gained in its structural adjustment. In the course of implementing regional strategies, namely, those so-called strategies of "Go-West," of "Rejuvenation Northeast China and Other Old Industrial Bases," and of "Rise of the Central Regions," the central government has used various policy measures to encourage favorable and subsidized investments in the central and western regions. While this policy has reduced regional disparities by artificially counterpoising investments in infrastructure and industries among the eastern, central, and western regions, the subsidies and favorable loans have obliterated the distinction between competitive and inefficient investments. Those investments deviating from the comparative advantages in the central and western regions lead to heavy reliance of some enterprises on policy support. From 2000 to 2007, the annual growth rates of the capital–labor ratios in central and western provinces on average were 9.2% and 8.1%, respectively, much higher than the average growth rate of 4.2% in eastern provinces. In 2007, the capital–labor ratios in the central and western regions were 20.1% and 25.9% higher than that in eastern regions, respectively (Cai *et al.*, 2009).

Second, the labor shortage and wage convergence between unskilled and skilled workers tends to create a disincentive for schooling and to weaken human capital accumulation in the near future. The accelerating structural change in China's economy is heightening the demand for work skills that are supposed to be accumulated through education and training. The rapid growth in the demand for unskilled labor and resulting increase in the wages of unskilled workers, however, temporarily weakens a family's motivation to have their children stay in schools, since they now face better employment opportunities and higher pay in the labor market, and increased opportunity costs of schooling.

As is shown in previous studies, an overwhelming portion of the urban sectors' need for labor has been fulfilled by labor migration from rural areas, and while human capital endowments of rural migrant workers are relatively lower, they have been increasing over time (Wang, 2009). If the human capital accumulation process is halted, even temporarily, it will not only encumber the structural upgrade of the Chinese industry, but it will also generate difficulty of employment for some groups of workers in the near future. To avert such a risk, government intervention in subsidizing secondary education, vocational education, and on-job-training is urgently needed and highly appropriate.

Building labor market institutions

Although a meeting between the Lewis turning point and lagged Kuznets turning point can be expected by theory and was confirmed by the experiences in some countries, the improvement of the income distribution is not as spontaneous as the arrival of the Lewis turning point, but instead is conditional on institutional arrangements in both domains of primary distribution and redistribution. The advent of the Lewis turning point changes the relationship between demand for and supply of labor market institutions, giving rise to public policies that are favorable toward ordinary workers and low-income families in the labor market.

As laborers, especially the migrant workers in the Chinese case, they face more employment opportunities and actually obtain the power to "exit" or the rights to "vote with their feet." How they use such a power depends on what jobs they currently hold. For example, they may simply choose to quit if they are not satisfied with a job in a small, futureless enterprise, since they now have plentiful outside options for employment. Also, they are more likely to take actions to voice their concerns in front of employers, such as filing complaints, engaging in collective bargaining, and even organizing strikes in order to seek higher pay and better working conditions, if they are dissatisfied with their current status, but reluctant to leave the firms. In recent years, particularly after 2008 when the Chinese labor laws were updated, labor disputes have intensified. This is not a sign of worsening labor relations, but an indication of stronger demand for labor market institutions.

After their economies arrived at the Lewis turning point, Japan and Korea used different approaches to deal with the increased demand for higher wages. When Japan arrived at its turning point around 1960 (Minami, 1968), the government seriously responded to labor disputes by playing an active role in collective bargaining and helped form harmonious labor relations. As a result, the income distribution quickly improved after the arrival of the Lewis turning point, and Japan became the country with the least income inequality (see Minami, 1998; Moriguchi and Saez, 2008). In Korea, when it arrived at its turning point around 1970, the role of trade unions was still restricted by the government and workers did not feel satisfied with their wages. The consequence was not only a slower improvement of its income distribution compared to that of Japan's, but there was also a disastrous political cost, namely, more than a decade long collapse of social cohesion (see Freeman, 1993). In short, the time lag between the Lewis turning point and Kuznets turning point was much longer in Korea than in Japan, because of different approaches in building labor market institutions.

Fostering new consumers

Turning ordinary workers and low-income families, who benefit the most from increased wages and the convergence of wages occurring at the Lewis turning point, into new consumers, is critical for transforming Chinese growth from being export- and investment-driven into being consumption-driven. Migrant workers should be the primary focus of this concern. While they work and live in cities, migrant workers cannot normally spend what they earn, like their native counterparts do, for two reasons. First, without urban *hukou*, they are not well covered by urban social security programs. Second, their employment is unsecured and they are thus subjected to cyclical unemployment.

According to a study conducted by the Asian Development Bank (Chun, 2010), the Chinese middle class, namely, those whose daily income is between 2 and 20 USD, while making up 66% of the total population, contributes to 79.2% of total consumption of China. The same study categorizes the Chinese middle class into three groups: the lower middle class with a daily income between 2 and 4 USD; the mid middle class with a daily income between 4 and 10 USD; and higher middle class with a daily income between 10 and 20 USD. Based on such a categorization, we find that the rural households, whose average daily income is 3.6 USD, the migrant households, whose average daily income is 9.4 USD, and urban resident households, whose daily income is 11.9 USD, fall into lower, mid and higher middle class groups, respectively. That is, not only can poverty alleviation increase a household's consumption level, but labor mobility, and more significantly the attainment of urban citizenship, can increase consumption levels. In this case, when households escape poverty, namely, when daily income jumps from lower than 1.25 USD to 1.25 to 2 USD, their consumption increases by 120.5%. When households enter the lower middle class, their consumption increases by 17.5%. When rural households migrate and become migrant households, their consumption increases by 80.1%. When migrant households get urban *hukou*, their consumption increases by 117.8%.

Chapter 4

Employment Challenges After Reaching the Lewis Turning Point

4.1. Increased Urgency of Employment Challenges in the Long Term

My colleagues and I have predicted that China's labor shortage will occur between 2004 and 2009. Evidence shows that the "peasant worker shortage" was highlighted in 2004, and the aggravation of labor shortage in 2009 was delayed after the spring festival because of the financial crisis's short-term impact. It can be inferred that the recent nationwide labor shortage is the continuation of the long-term changes of labor market landscape that first appeared in 2004. The shortage of and the wage rate increase of unskilled labor are the obvious signals and undeniable evidence of the arrival of the Lewis turning point.

Reaching the Lewis turning point does not imply that the employment difficulty can be immediately solved but rather indicates that the employment problem has been transformed from aggregate issues to structural ones. In other words, the long-term employment problem that labor supply exceeds labor demand is replaced by the cyclical unemployment which is affected by macroeconomic conditions, and the structural and frictional unemployment which arises from mismatches between specific groups' employment needs and the labor market demand. Since the arrival of the Lewis turning point indicates a phase change of the long-term economic growth, China faces employment challenges both in the short term and in the long term, and it is more urgent in the long run than in the short run.

Emerging non-aggregate employment difficulties

Employment difficulties in China have long since been related to the characteristic that aggregate labor supply exceeds aggregate labor demand, reflected as abundant surplus labor in the rural areas, enterprise redundancy in the urban areas, and highlighted unemployment problems. The employment difficulty is highlighted in the insufficient number of jobs, in the special periods such as during the reform that broke "the iron bowls," or when experiencing the labor market shocks when jobs lost exceeded those created. During these periods, the economic growth that helped create jobs for average workers, the institutional reforms that promoted the labor market development, and government efforts that assisted laid-off workers for reemployment made up the main contents of the proactive employment policies.

Acute demographic transition and high-speed economic growth have fundamentally changed the relationship of labor supply and labor demand in recent years. On one hand, the growth of labor supply has slowed over the years, it is predicted that the working-age population aged between 16 and 64 years will stop increasing in 2013. Before that time, its growth rate has gradually decreased and its increment has declined by 13.6% annually between 2004 and 2011. On the other hand, high speed economic growth has created a strong labor demand and the peasant worker shortage has spread all over the country since 2004, despite a short pause because of the financial crisis. Using the incremental working-age population as the labor supply and the incremental urban employment (including peasant workers) as the labor demand, we will find that the characteristic that labor supply exceeds labor demand no longer exists in the labor market of China (Figure 4.1).

However, the employment pressure is not reduced with the large scale of rural labor migrating to the urban areas, and the relief of the aggregate contradiction between labor supply and labor demand occurred with the urban employment structural adjustments. In fact, the manifestation of the cyclical, structural, and frictional unemployment or employment difficulties is only the tip of the iceberg. Behind are deeper structural problems. The temporary return of peasant workers during the financial crisis and the succeeding severe peasant worker shortage reveal that agriculture is no longer the reservoir of surplus labor, urban areas have rigid demand for peasant workers, and peasant workers are no longer the marginal urban

Increment of Labor Supply and Labor Demand
(in Ten Thousands)

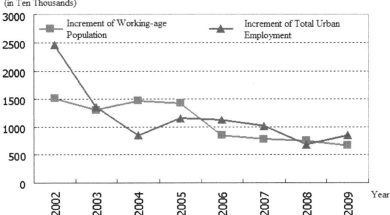

Figure 4.1. New Trend in the Relationship of Labor Supply and Labor Demand.

Source: The Statistical Yearbook of China (all previous years), *The Yearbook of China's Rural Household Survey* (all previous years) and *The Demographic Yearbook of China* (all previous years).

workers who "migrate in and out" of the urban areas. In the meantime, peasant workers have not become legitimate permanent urban residents and are not covered by the social security system; therefore, they will face the cyclical unemployment problem in the long term. In 2010, there were 150 million migrant peasant workers, 95% of which worked in the urban areas and were the targeted group of employment policies.

The demand for human capital in the long term

With changes in the relationship between labor supply and labor demand, the employment problem of college graduates has become more acute. According to relevant statistics and investigations, the employment rate of college graduates did not improve, and even decreased, in 2010, when the labor shortage emerged. It can be inferred that the employment difficulty that they face is not the problem of aggregate job positions, but the contradiction between their job expectations and skills and the demand of the labor market. Generally speaking, workers with higher education levels have more specific human capital, which increases the difficulty of matching them with the labor market demand. Because the endowments of college graduates are their comprehensive knowledge and specific skills, whether their human capital and job expectations match the labor market demand determines their employment outcomes and unemployment risks.

Unemployed urban residents are another targeted group of employment policies. They become a vulnerable group in the labor market, with the typical characteristics of relatively weak human capital, old age, low education level, poor health condition, and lack of skills, especially the capability to update their knowledge and skills. A large portion of the registered urban unemployment that only covers urban residents with local registration statistically belongs to this group. They are affected by cyclical factors, but their employment difficulties have more persistent natural unemployment characteristics. For example, no matter the financial crisis shocks in 2009 or the significant employment recovery in 2010, the registered unemployment rate, which reflects employment difficulties of and shocks on urban residents, did not fluctuate very much. Registered unemployed urban population steadily stayed at around 13 million.

There are mainly the human-capital-related structural factors and the labor-market-function-related frictional factors that affect the employment of college graduates and unemployed urban residents, which are generally called the natural unemployment factors. For college graduates, the key point is to match their professional skills with the labor market demand. For unemployed urban residents, the fundamental reason for their weak position in the labor market is their low education levels and lack of skills. Therefore, it is very difficult to deal with the problem because the natural employment difficulty and unemployment risks still exist, even when the aggregate relationship between labor supply and labor demand is improved.

Therefore, a long-term problem of China's employment policies is whether the human capital satisfies the labor market demand. From Chinese workers' education levels, education years decrease 10.2% on average as age increases one year for workers aged between 24 and 64 years. The trend of decreasing education years becomes more obvious when a worker's age increases: education years decrease 16.1% on average as age increases one year for workers between 44 and 64 years. Assume that there is a critical minimum human capital level and the critical minimum level is nine years (with the compulsory education requirements), then the critical population is aged 33 years in China's working-age population. Workers above this age will often face structural and frictional employment and reemployment barriers before their retirement. Therefore, in this new trend, proactive employment policies should include not only job creation, but, as a more important and challenging long-term task, improve the working skills for workers, including peasant workers, college graduates, and urban residents.

More urgent challenge in the long term

With the arrival of the Lewis turning point that is reflected in the new relationship of labor supply and labor demand, especially after the economic recovery from the financial crisis, China's employment situation has been significantly improved. Correspondingly, China should not be trapped in the short-term aggregate employment contradictions. However, the long-lasting labor human capital problem will become a factor that restricts not only the sustainable economic growth but also the employment expansion in the current and future labor market. Therefore, it is more urgent to deal with the challenge in the long term than in the short term.

After reaching the Lewis turning point, China's economy will face more problems; which have troubled many market economy countries, including some "growing pains" and challenges that some developed economies have encountered. For example, after the high-speed economic growth for almost 20 years, Japan approached the Lewis turning point in the early-1960s, lost demographic dividend after 1990, and was trapped in the "lost 10 years" (lost 20 years so far). According to economists Fumio Hayashi and Edward Prescott's researches, Japan's economic stagnation in this period was due to its poor total factor productivity performance. For another example, the U.S. experienced jobless recoveries after several economic recessions in the 1990s, i.e., the cycle for employment recovering to the level before the recession became longer after the economy started to recover. This sets a new record in the recent financial crisis: the jobless recovery will last 10 years, according to economists' predictions. This phenomenon is directly related to the facts that average workers' human capital did not catch up with the industry structural upgrade and average workers cannot adapt to the new job requirements in the U.S. For example, the unemployment rate of workers without a college degree is three times of that of college graduates.

After China's economy reached the Lewis turning point, it is very urgent to change the economic development pattern, with the focus on transforming the driving force of economic growth from the increase of production input factors to the increase of total factor productivity. In the meantime, with China's industrialization stepping into a higher stage, the production input endowments structure will see tremendous changes and the industry structural upgrade will accelerate. All of these factors bring higher requirements for the labor human capital. However, in conditions of the average worker shortage and the continual wage increase, it is easy to generate the negative incentive for rural students to drop out of school and hurriedly seek jobs, leaving future human capital deficits. If adequate quantity of labor (demographic dividends) is the main resource of the economic growth before reaching the turning point, then the future sustainable economic growth will rely more on human capital and workers' working skills (second demographic dividends). Therefore, it is urgent to solve the problem of the long-term human capital accumulation. We should plan the policies ahead and solve the problems as soon as we can.

4.2. The Implication of Wage Convergence in the Urban Labor Market

A new phenomenon exists in the urban labor market: the first-time employment wage rate of many college graduates and the wage rate of urban reemployed workers have a tendency to decrease. In the meantime, the wage rate of migrant peasant workers tends to increase. Therefore, the wage rates of three different worker groups in the labor market are converging.

Wage differences and distortions

Workers' human capital endowments, such as educational background, working experience, and skills, varies, therefore, the existence of wage differences is a normal phenomenon in the labor market. However, if systematic wage differences caused by factors other than demographic characteristics exist among different groups of workers, then it implies discrimination in the labor market. Through econometric analysis, many researchers found that there exist such systematic wage differences between peasant workers and local resident workers. For example, a research shows that the average wage rate of peasant workers is lower than the wage rate of local resident workers by one fourth and only 30–40% of such a wage gap can be explained by the difference in education levels between migrant workers and local resident workers, which implies that it is caused by discrimination.

Therefore, it is natural to raise the following question: Are peasant workers paid less or are wages for local resident workers artificially set high? Following the economic principles, in a labor market without distortions, workers should receive the wage rate that is equal to their marginal product of labor. Researchers found that in China's labor market, the peasant workers' marginal product of labor is 3.86 times their wage rate, while local resident workers' marginal product of labor is 80.5% of their wage rate. This means that peasant workers are paid less, because their marginal product of labor is higher than their wage rate and local resident workers' wage rate is too high because their marginal product of labor is lower than their wage rate.

Wage convergence and its implications

Therefore, it is not surprising to see the emergence of the new phenomenon that the wage rates of the three groups of workers in the labor market (peasant workers, reemployed workers, and college graduates) are converging.

First of all, the wage rate of peasant workers tends to increase. The wage rate of peasant workers has been kept low for a long time, which has gained broad concerns in society. An investigation conducted in 2004 shows that the average monthly wage rate of peasant workers in the Pearl River Delta region is only 600 Yuan, which is the same as their wage rate 10 years ago. However, with the emerging "peasant worker shortage" in the coastal areas and its spread to the labor exporting areas, peasant workers' wages are rising at an unprecedented rate, so much so that the increment in 2005 exceeded the total increment in the past 10 years.

Second, the wage rate of reemployed workers is lower than what they used to receive before their lay-offs. After experiencing market shocks, such as seniority buyout, lay-off, and early retirement, urban workers are able to find jobs again. As their job position changes, their wage rate is sharply declining and approaching to the level that peasant workers are receiving.

Lastly, the first-time employment wage rate of college graduates has significantly declined. Irrespective of the labor market guiding prices, higher educational institutes' follow-up investigations to its graduates or surveys on graduates' expected wages show that the first-time employment wage rate of college graduates has sharply declined. Despite the extreme hype of the "zero-wage employment," etc., it is not rare that college graduates are employed with a monthly wage rate lower than 1000 Yuan. This change in the labor market shows that there used to be distortions in the wage difference among different groups of workers and the event that is taking place is a correction of the distortions. The fact of wage convergence between migrant workers and urban vulnerable workers is well understandable, because the reemployed workers who have experienced the unemployment shocks are relatively old, lack skills, are poorly educated, and do not have human capital advantage over peasant workers who are relatively young and mainly middle school graduates. Why do highly educated college graduates join the wage convergence?

On one hand, there is the matching problem in the labor market. Enrollment expansion and the rapid development in higher education is not accompanied with corresponding education institutional reforms, and the education system and mechanisms such as major settings, course contents, and graduate placements, have not adapted to the labor market. With mismatches between their skills and the labor market demand, graduates cannot find jobs that suit their professional trainings and have to look for jobs out of their specialized fields. Under this condition, college graduates have no obvious human capital advantage over the other groups of workers.

On the other hand, there is the education quality problem in higher educational institutes. In the condition that not every college graduate can find a job in their specialized fields, colleges and universities can greatly enhance their graduates' competitiveness in the labor market if they can significantly improve students' universal skills such as knowing a foreign language, acquiring computer skills, and developing management capabilities. However, many colleges and universities blindly expand enrollment without adequate preparation of teachers and teaching facilities and cause declining education quality. College graduates have to compete in the lower-end of the labor market if they cannot fulfill their narrow professional skills. However, one cannot blame on the enrollment expansion of higher education; in fact, a large portion of college graduates still receive wages that are several times higher than what peasant workers receive, particularly after a few years from their graduation.

Implications and policy suggestions

As a correction to the previous distortions, the wage convergence of different groups of workers in the labor market provides an important implication for the reform: we can achieve the goal of reducing unjustified wage differentials not only by increasing wages for lower-end worker groups in absolute term but also by depressing wages for higher-end worker groups in relative term, i.e., both methods of addition and subtraction should be applied. The labor market reform shows that China can use specific incremental adjustments for different groups to achieve the goal of the reform with relatively low compensation costs and without sacrificing the stability.

Since the wage convergence is a correction to the labor market distortions, it implies that interventions to this process would be untimely and contract the spirit of the reform. In other words, it is the labor market that leads the wage rates of both college students and reemployed workers to decline. Administrative interventions must be avoided at this time, and any attempt to protect these two groups, even with good intentions, would eventually be detrimental to the employment of these two groups if the labor market functions were damaged during the intervention. This does not mean that the government and society can do nothing. From the aspect of policy guide and public services, the government and society should enhance the construction of the social security system and social protection mechanisms according to the current informal employment trend in the labor market and construct an efficient employment and reemployment training system according to the new characteristic of larger labor mobility in the future. In addition, relevant departments should cooperate to construct a labor market-led education system to fix its mal-adaptation to the labor market demand.

4.3. Promoting Healthy Development of China's Labor Market

In 2009, China realized rapid economic growth, while the employment of urban and rural residents continually expanded. There even emerged the "peasant worker shortage" around the spring festival in 2010. Under the background of the global financial crisis, the labor market continued experiencing dramatic changes from surplus labor supply to labor shortage in the short term, which reflects the coexistence of opportunities and challenges in China today. Employment is an important factor that affects both economic growth and peoples' livelihoods. During the intersection of the first and second decades of the 21st century, it is the key moment for China to change the economic growth pattern and adjust the economic structure, so the healthy development of China's labor market can be more closely conformed to the new stage of development.

Recognition of China's urban employment situation

Although the financial crisis had a relatively light impact on China's economy, enterprises in the coastal areas and the export-oriented and labor-intensive industries were inevitably affected by declining exports, and with the effect of China's macroeconomic policy factors, a large amount of peasant workers lost jobs. However, during only several months in the first half of 2009, tens of millions of migrant peasant workers first returned home, and 95% of them then returned to cities and 97% of them found jobs, where the aggregate quantity of peasant workers increased by 4.59 million and the "peasant worker shortage" emerged again. This fully reflected the fluctuation process of the occurrence, responses, and adjustments of employment shocks.

On one hand, large-scale labor migration and urban employment institutional reforms since the initiation of the reform and opening-up policies gradually eliminate the surplus labor in the rural areas and the enterprise redundancy in the urban areas, therefore, institutional unemployment has gradually disappeared. On the other hand, China successfully dealt with the financial crisis, and the economy started to recover and the cyclical unemployment is back to the normal level.

With the declining surplus labor and the arrival of the Lewis turning point, institutional unemployment has gradually disappeared in China. Effective macroeconomic policies help to free China out of the financial crisis and the cyclical unemployment population has decreased. However, an open market economy will inevitably experience economic fluctuations and the cyclical unemployment problem will return. Therefore, the cyclical unemployment rate should become the basis for making macroeconomic policies. Restricted by the labor market development level, the structure of human capital development and the labor market demand for human capital is asymmetric and the natural unemployment problem will gradually become the major issue in the labor market. College graduates face inconsistencies between their skills and the labor market demand; urban unemployed residents are restricted with relatively low education levels and young peasant workers cannot adapt to the changing industrial structure. The focus of future employment policies should extend to education and trainings with the primary goal of lowering the natural unemployment rate.

The in-depth reason for the employment fluctuation of peasant workers

Japan approached the Lewis turning point in the 1960s when there was a high influx of peasant workers into cities. Later, the cyclical unemployment did not lead migrant workers to return to rural areas and the labor market was adjusted through the service industry, which absorbed a large number of workers. How did China adjust the labor market during the financial crisis?

Labor transfer is irreversible because migrant workers have not been needed in agricultural productions for a long time, while peasant workers are indispensable in the urban areas because labor demand for peasant workers has been rigid. When labor supply exceeds labor demand, the cyclical labor demand changes in urban or non-agricultural industries usually caused the labor quantity in agriculture to change in the opposite direction, which meant that the employment scale in agriculture is not determined by its own demand and agriculture is still the reservoir of surplus labor. However, when approaching the turning point of supply and demand, labor demand fluctuations in urban areas and non-agricultural industries seldom cause opposite labor quantity changes in agriculture. On one hand, agriculture no longer has the function to absorb surplus labor, and on the other hand, urban areas and non-agricultural industries are more capable to adjust the short run changes in labor supply and demand. This results in agriculture no longer being the reservoir of surplus labor.

The processes of economic recovery and the peasant worker employment adjustment occurred as follows: facing the shock of declining exports, the primary sector that absorbs labor has changed from the manufacturing industry to the service industry. In addition, there are also many new employment opportunities in the construction industry after the implementation of the fiscal stimulus package. Compared to the normal investment structure in previous years, the investment portfolio package provided by the National Development and Reform Committee further reflects the challenge from declining exports and structural adjustments. Investment reduced from normal share of 45% to stimulus share of 7% in the manufacturing industry, increases from 46% to 76% in the construction industry, and from 9% to 17% in the service industry. Overall, such a stimulus investment portfolio could enhance the employment absorption capability by 15%. Obviously, the fiscal stimulus package is making great efforts to increase peasant workers' employment and reemployment and realizing the employment structural adjustment, all together.

Since the beginning of 21st century, state budget has been inclined to investment in agriculture, rural areas, and central and western regions, which has greatly increased the employment opportunities for migrant rural workers. With the industrial, urban and rural, and regional development, a large amount of labor demand is created. In addition, since China successfully dealt with the financial crisis, labor-intensive industries were least shocked, recovered relatively early, and first created employment demand. In the condition that peasant workers were almost completely absorbed, the reaccelerating economic growth inevitably encountered the "peasant worker shortage."

How China deals with the problem of "growing old before becoming rich"

Worldwide experiences show that the main driving force of demographic transition is economic growth and social development. China's high-speed economic growth miracle has lasted for over 30 years after the reform and opening-up initiated in the late 1970s, but it started later than the "Four Tigers" in Asia, therefore, the problem of "growing old before becoming rich" emerged when China stepped into the new demographic transition period with relatively low income per capita.

Although they all face the aging population challenge for the economic growth and pension insurance system, developed countries have different levels of effectiveness in dealing with the aging population problem. Overall, these countries have relatively high income per capita and advanced technological innovations, so their economic growth, which is mainly driven by productivity, is sustainable and sufficient to deal with the aging population crisis.

Correspondingly, the key for China to handle the demographic transition consequences — namely, the decreasing working-age population and higher demographic aging level, is to maintain high-speed economic growth. Higher income per capita and stronger state economic power will enable China to strengthen the social security system, especially the pension system as well as the social capability of supporting and assisting elderly people. With the closure of gap between "growing old" and "becoming rich," the industrial structure will better adapt to the resource endowments structure and economic growth will become more sustainable, less relying on production input factors, and less restricted to the labor shortage.

China's world ranking in aggregate economic volume continuously increases, population growth rate greatly declines, and the growth of GDP per capita accelerates. From the second decade of the 21st century, China will accelerate its transition from a middle-income country to a high-income country. Therefore, the gap between the economic growth level and the population aging level will gradually decrease.

When achieving the goal of constructing a well-being society and reaching (or getting close to) the income per capita levels in developed countries in 2020, China will be able to obtain the advantage of backwardness in institutional development in the face of the aging population challenge. Therefore, sufficiently exploiting the potential of the current demographic dividends, creating new demographic dividends, and gradually utilizing the new economic growth resources are the primary ways to deal with the aging population problem after reaching the Lewis turning point.

Understanding the changing trend in China's labor cost advantage

China's GDP will exceed USD 5.4 trillion in 2010, predicting that China will exceed Japan as the second largest economy in the world. In the meantime, China's income per capita level is still among the middle-income countries. This implies that China's economy will step into the development stage of "growing big before becoming rich." China's central and western regions face a similar situation. In the recent decade, the economic growth in the central and western regions has been faster than that in the east regions, implying that the aggregate economic volume in the central and western regions will increase. However, the income per capita level in the central regions is just above half of that in the eastern regions and the income per capita level in the western regions is just 44% of that in the eastern regions. The problem of "growing big before becoming rich" also exists in China's central and western regions.

As a sizeable economy and a large country in international trade, China will face more trade conflicts in the future, since both developed countries and developing countries tend to implement trade protections mainly against China. Therefore, China should prepare early in order to confidently react to the situation in the future. In the meantime, the country should use the regional difference to build the domestic "flying-geese" model. For industries that have lost the comparative advantage in the coastal areas because of increasing costs, China should transfer them to the central and western regions to succeed in the comparative advantage that is gradually lost in the east regions, and China should obtain shares in the international market for export-oriented and labor-intensive industries to gradually reduce regional differences. China has to realize the transition of the economic growth pattern and its comparative advantage in the international market with the help of free trade and economic globalization. After experiencing the growth period that highly relies on external demands, China will quickly increase residents' incomes, improve urban and rural income distributions, develop residents' consumption capabilities, and realize the transition of the economic growth pattern. In so doing, we may need to answer the following questions.

First of all, will the global economy continue to support China as the manufacturing center? The core of the global economy rebalancing currently occurring worldwide, is to increase the saving rate in the U.S. and the domestic consumption in the emerging economies through a series of adjustments. The "rebalancing" is mainly concerned with the competitive advantage and market share of China's manufacturing products, and thus China's future trading environment will be more complicated because of the various "rebalancing" efforts. However, the fact of the high labor costs of developed countries and the inability to resume the comparative advantage in labor-intensive manufacturing products is fateful and irreversible. The realization of the "global economy rebalancing" will eventually rely on the development of Chinese residents' consumption capability. With the employment expansion and improvements in residents' incomes and income distributions, China's domestic consumption demand will significantly increase and gradually replace the foreign demand. At that point, China will become a huge consumer market.

Second, will China lose its comparative advantage to other developing countries, such as India, Vietnam, or Mexico? Some research reports point out that China is losing its position as the world's manufacturing center because of the rapidly increasing costs, having been and/or will be replaced by those countries. The finding, however, is not accurate since China will still keep its comparative advantage in labor-intensive manufacturing industries for a substantial period. Because of the unbalanced regional developments, China can keep the advantage of low labor cost, build the "flying-geese" model among the east, central, and west regions through policy adjustments, and its labor-intensive manufacturing industries will continue to develop in the next 10 to 20 years. In addition, competitiveness comes not only from the wage cost, but also from the labor productivity. In fact, the growth of the labor productivity in China's manufacturing industries was fast enough to match the growth of wage rate and was the fastest in the world in the past several years.

Finally, is it a contradiction to continue to rely on exports and to transit to the domestic demand-oriented development pattern? There is no contradiction between them. The domestic demand expansion is the result of increased income per capita and the income increase relies on the employment expansion and free rural labor migration. Therefore, China should first rely on the employment-promoting economic growth. To keep the export-oriented industrial structure for a certain period is the important guarantee for sufficient employment of peasant workers and, therefore, is the must-follow route for reducing the urban and rural income differentials and improving the overall income distribution. Since the current urban and rural household income statistics neglects the income increase from labor migration, people not only overestimate the levels of income differentials and income inequality but also overlook the huge effect of labor migration and sufficient employment on the improvement of income distributions. In addition, to expand employment in the central and western regions is of great importance for raising residents' income levels and stimulating domestic consumption demand in those regions.

4.4. Extended Reading: Growing Pains: What Employment Dilemma Does China Face at its Lewisian Turning Point?

Introduction

According to Lewisian classical theory of economic development, developing countries characterized by an unlimited supply of labor are bound for a dual economy development. Namely, the modern sector can obtain endless transformed labor from the agricultural sector at constant wage rates and form its capital accumulation (Lewis, 1954). Therefore, the employment pressure caused by labor supply exceeding labor demand characterizes the entire process of such development. When the development of a dual economy moves to a stage at which labor demand of the modern sector exceeds labor supply originated from an agricultural surplus labor force at the present wage rate, it reaches an important turning point — the Lewisian turning point (Lewis, 1972). While this theory has held prevalence in many developing countries and among development economists, little has so far been studied and agreed upon regarding where major changes would occur and what challenges a country faces when it approaches such a turning point. This paper attempts to fill that knowledge gap by generalizing the stylized facts on relevant experiences in China — namely, the experiences of passing through its Lewisian turning point.

Like in many newly industrialized economies in East Asia, China's rapid economic growth during the reform period has been accompanied by accelerated demographic transition — in particular, a transition from demographic patterns characterized by high birth rate, low mortality, and high growth rate of population to that characterized by low birth rate, low mortality, and low growth rate of population. In China, the total fertility rate declined to a level below the replacement rate as early as the 1990s and natural growth rate of population dropped to 5.05 per thousand in 2008. This sort of demographic transition usually brings about a change characterized by a process in which working-age population first rapidly grows, then experiences a slower growth, and eventually stops growing. The Chinese economy is still at its long-running boom, which accordingly leads to a strong demand for labor, therefore fundamental changes in the supply of and demand for labor profile have inevitably occurred.

The rapid economic growth has also been accompanied by tremendous economic and social transformation. As the institutional barriers deterring labor mobility gradually allowed for better labor migration from rural to urban sectors, the non-agricultural share of employment has significantly diminished in compliance with the general pathway of economic development. As the result of the employment system reform and labor market development in urban areas, which is a consistent part of the transition from a planning system to market mechanism, overstaffing in enterprises is phasing out and labor force is being allocated and adjusted by market force to a much larger extent. The human capital accumulation has also accelerated with fuller coverage of compulsory education programs, significant increase in senior high schooling, and expansion of higher education.

While the labor market development has dramatically altered the pattern of the supply of and demand for labor by expanding employment and improving quality of labor force, there emerged a host of intricate phenomena in the labor market, which has puzzled scholars and policy makers. This includes the coexistence of labor shortage and employment difficulty, in general, and the coexistence of the ease for migrant workers' employment and difficulty for university graduates' employment, and of the trend of tight labor market and difficulties facing vulnerable groups of labor market participants. Confronted with such a conflicting labor market manifestation, the government addresses it incompletely and scholars explain it inconsistently, which has deterred sound policy-making.

The dilemma in dealing with and understanding China's current labor market is mainly caused by the lack of consistent theoretical framework in analyzing it. While mainstream macroeconomics and labor economics are bound up in explaining the labor market phenomena under neoclassical assumptions, they are incapable of understanding the labor market phenomena under the condition of a dual economy characterized by an unlimited supply of labor. However, the Lewisian theory of dual economy is popular among Chinese scholars and policy researchers in analyzing economic development with an unlimited labor supply, but it inevitably cuts itself off, because it can hardly be synchronized with the basic assumptions and analytical framework of mainstream economics. Once the Chinese economy enters into its Lewisian turning point, at which point the characteristics of dual economy are joined by those of neoclassical economy, neither paradigm alone helps in understanding the phenomena occurring in the labor market.

Starting with revealing the changes in labor market, this section attempts to integrate macroeconomics and labor economics with development economics to form a coherent analytical framework in order to explore the new features of the labor market as a result from the development of dual economy and system reform. It then indicates the demand of all labor market participants for labor market institutions and other arenas of social protection and emerging characteristics of the institutional supply originating from the transformation of government function. Based on studies in this section, some policy suggestions are proposed in the conclusion.

The Properties of Emerging Problems in the Labor Market

The most obvious manifestation of China's new phase of demographic transition is its changed age structure brought on by a stretch of low fertility rate. The dramatic decline in total fertility rate (TFR) in China — namely, a drop from 5.8 to 2.3 — occurred during the 1970s, as well as a slow continuous decline after 1980. Now it is commonly believed to range between 1.6 and 1.8. The long-lasting, low fertility rate gives rise to a change in population age structure. Since 1980, the growth of the aged

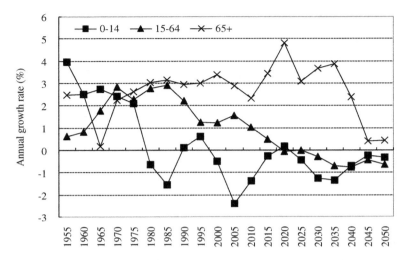

Figure 4.2. Growth Rates of Chinese Population by Age Group.
Source: United Nations (2009).

population has accelerated, the growth of the working-age population has rapidly slowed, and the growth of the youth population has shrunk (Figure 4.2). The implication of such demographic dynamics is the long-standing low fertility leading to an inadequacy of labor supply as the working-age population first slows its growth and eventually stop growing. According to an updated prediction (United Nations, 2009), the year 2015 is China's turning point at which the population, aged 15 to 64 years, will stop increasing and subsequently begin shrinking.

This changing trend of the working-age population, however, hardly helps one understand the status quo of the labor market because it disregards required new jobs made by government department during employment changes. That is, while according to the prediction, the increment of the working-age population has never been more than 20 million, the officially claimed number of new jobs needed each year to meet the employment need of the newly emerging labor force has always been larger. The balance formula used by the Ministry of Human Resources and Social Security includes the following components and equates to a potential supply of labor force exceeding 24 million: (1) Over 10 million

Beyond Demographic Dividend

new labor market entrants; (2) Over eight million unemployed who need jobs; and (3) Over six million laid-off workers who demand jobs (Zhang, 2008, p. 323).

This estimation is problematic. First of all, this estimation has no time structure. Such a parlance has continued for many years and has never been altered in accordance with the different labor supply and demand situation. In fact, there are no longer laid-off workers; after 2005, they were converted into the category of registered unemployment, which totaled 80 million in 2008. Second, it intends to absorb all the unemployed, which is neither necessary nor feasible. As will be explained below, natural unemployment is usually persistent and its level in the labor market is relatively stable.

Examining the various sources on China's migration (urban employment and population prediction), one can find that the sum of the increment of migrant workers and increment of urban employment each year is indeed larger than the increment of the working-age population in recent years. Given the inconsistency of employment statistics in terms of definition, categorization, and coverage and especially the existence of a large proportion of informal employment missing from official statistics (Cai, 2004), it is practically impossible to formulate a balance sheet between laborers supplied and laborers employed. Thus, we give up the intention and instead try to build an imbalance sheet based on available data. This can still help us understand the status quo of China's labor market.

In Table 4.1, we show the data imbalance of labor supplied and used by listing an accurate prediction on the increment of the working-age population, the increment of cross-region migrant workers, and increment of urban local employment. It is worth noting that if we consider the increment of the working-age population as a proxy of labor supply, the increment of cross-region migrant workers and increment of urban local employment as a sum of labor utilization, the imbalance revealed in the table conflicts with government claims every year. That is, instead of a situation of supply exceeding demand for labor, we actually witness a situation of demand exceeding supply of labor.

The difference between the sum incremental amount of migrant workers and urban employees and the incremental amount of the working-age

Table 4.1.   Increments of Working-Age Population and of Employment (Million).

	Working population (1)	**Migrant workers (2)**	**Urban employment (3)**	**Absorbed hidden unemployment (4)***
2002	15.11	20.71	8.40	−14.00
2003	13.05	9.20	8.59	−4.74
2004	14.70	4.33	8.37	2.00
2005	1436	7.55	8.55	−1.74
2006	8.54	6.34	9.79	−7.59
2007	7.82	4.85	10.40	−7.43
2008	7.54	3.44	8.60	−4.50
2009	6.65	4.59	11.02	−8.96

* (4) = (1) − [(2) + (3)].

Source: Data of working age population is based on estimation by Hu (2009); data on migrant workers is from NBS-DORSES (various years), the 2009 figure is from NDRC (2010).

population consists of the following components: First, while the majority of the cross-region migrant workers enter cities, some of them may work at township and village enterprises (TVEs). Since the detailed distribution of TVEs' workers is unknown, this factor impacts the understanding of the balance of labor demand and supply; second, the residual workers mainly consist of hidden unemployed laborers, which were in the stock of working-age population and manifested as a surplus labor force in rural sectors and overstaffing in urban sectors. Temporarily, these reallocated workers are called the "absorbed hidden unemployment."

The trends of the labor market can be further investigated through three major labor groups: First, the changing trend and characteristics of migrant workers are examined. As is shown in Table 4.1, in spite of massive migration from rural to urban areas in the early 2000s, its growth rate and incremental amount have been diminishing, which is consistent with the diminishing growth of the rural working-age population. The adjustment process of the labor market during the global financial crisis showed the emerged characteristics of rural labor migration. That is, the agricultural production mode has been changed in response to the massive rural migration to the urban sector. Agriculture is no longer a pool of surplus labor force, and the urban sectors' demand for migrant labor has become inelastic (Cai, 2010b). The adjustment process of migrant workers'

employment during the global financial crisis has validated those fundamental changes in the nature of the labor market. During this time,
migrant workers first returned home in early 2009 and came back to cities
right after the Chinese New Year holiday, and then a subsequent labor
shortage in the second half of the year became widespread after the 2010
Chinese New Year.

We can also observe the changing trends of urban employment. As is
shown in Table 4.1, the expansion of urban employment has been fast and
stable since the beginning of this century, and the amount of new employees increases every year at the enlarged base of total employment. The
contrasting trends between the increase in employment and diminishing
growth of the working-age population imply that the increment of urban
employment, to a certain extent, comes from urban labor force relocation.
That is, the redundant workers under planning systems first experienced
unemployment, and then became gradually reemployed. In fact, during
the period from 2002 to 2007 — namely, in the time span between the
recovery from the East Asian financial crisis in the late 1990s and beginning of 2008–2009 global financial crisis, the urban unemployment rate
decreased regularly. Meanwhile, many of those reemployed, mostly aged
40–50, are in a bind in the labor market, frequently become unemployed,
and face increasing difficulties of reemployment.

Third, we look into a special group of labor market participants — university graduates. As one of the countermeasures to cope with the labor
market shock in the late 1990s, an expansionary policy of higher education enrollment was initiated in 1999 and has been implemented since
then. In the period of 1998 to 2008, the annual growth rate of enrolled
students was 18.8%, 13.9 percentage points higher than the annual growth
rate of 4.9% in 1988 to 1998. The total enrollment of universities and colleges reached 6.08 million in 2008. While such a substantial expansion of
higher education does not add an extra amount of entrants to labor market,
it has indeed changed the composition of the labor force's educational
attainments, and those who hold higher degrees have a much higher
expectation for employment. The sudden expansion of university graduates and the mismatching of skills between what they learn and what the
labor market needs make the employment of graduates a main focus of the
government and society.

Unemployment Types and Their Trends in Transition

Two unemployment types — cyclical unemployment and natural unemployment (including frictional and structural unemployment) — draw major attention in macroeconomics and labor economics. Under the conditions of a typical market economy, as the macroeconomy fluctuates, the short-term relationship of labor demand and supply changes, giving rise to cyclical unemployment. Both the time costs of job searching and structural changes in demand for skills often lead to the mismatching of desires between job seekers and employers, causing natural unemployment of either a frictional or structural type. As the labor force becomes increasingly allocated through market mechanisms and the macroeconomy begins experiencing its business cycle, the Chinese labor market has witnessed cyclical unemployment and natural unemployment. According to an estimation (Cai *et al.*, 2004), in the period from 1995 to 2002, roughly 60–80% of the surveyed unemployed in urban China were not influenced by macroeconomy fluctuation and therefore can be viewed as natural unemployment.

Based on the ideas set forth by Lewis (1954), surplus labor persistently exists in agriculture and gradually shifts to non-agricultural sectors during the development of a dual economy. In the period between the mid-1980s and the late 1990s, it is commonly believed that 30–40% of China's agricultural laborers were surplus (Taylor, 1993; Carter *et al.*, 1996). Similarly, as a legacy of planning economy, the long accumulated redundant employees were then estimated to be as large as 30–40% of total employees in urban enterprises (Zhang, 2008, p. 101). Both these forms of underemployment in rural and urban sectors can be conceptualized as hidden unemployment.

We can conceptually divide the existing forms of unemployment and underemployment into cyclical unemployment, natural (frictional and structural) unemployment, and hidden unemployment and discuss their trends of change. The economic reforms in China started from a typical dual economy characterized by a sharp contrast between rural and urban areas, a large size, and high proportion of hidden unemployment widely existing in rural and urban sectors. At the same time, there exists natural unemployment due to underdevelopment of the labor market, lack of public employment services, mismatching of job skills, and cyclical

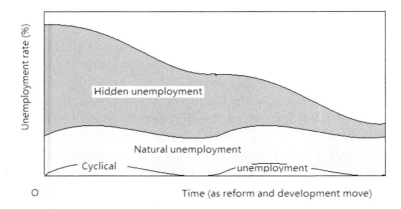

Figure 4.3.   Unemployment Types and Their Changing Trends as Reforms Deepen.

unemployment caused by macroeconomic fluctuation during the entire reform period. To clearly observe the reduction of hidden unemployment as the result of dual economy transformation, urban employment policy reform, and the break-up of enterprises' "iron rice bowl," we first assume that cyclical unemployment and natural unemployment are relatively constant.

From Figure 4.3, one can see that as the rural labor force continued migrating to urban areas and urban redundant workers became reallocated in the reform era, hidden unemployment substantially shrunk in terms of total size and its share in total unemployment. While disagreement remains, a host of empirical studies show that as the result of labor transfer from agricultural to non-agricultural sectors and from rural to urban areas, the amount and proportion of surplus labor in agriculture is significantly reduced (e.g., Cai and Wang, 2007; Zhang *et al.*, 2009). Since 2004, when labor shortage first appeared nationwide, wage rates of ordinary workers have constantly gone up, which is the sufficient evidence of Lewisian turning point arrival, in accordance with its definition.

After the late 1990s, the urban labor market experienced a painful adjustment, during which a cumulative 40 million workers were laid off. As labor markets developed and economic growth picked up, the laid-off and registered unemployed were either reemployed or chose to retire. As a result, the hidden urban unemployment group tends to be eliminated after experiencing such an adjustment, whereas those who are at older working ages frequently encounter unemployment shock due to frictional and structural causes.

Based on these recent trends, we are now in the position to answer a few difficult unemployment questions that emerged after the Lewis turning point arrived. They are: (1) Why migrant workers' employment is more volatile, (2) Why university graduates face bigger difficulties in finding jobs than less educated migrant workers, and (3) How workers at older working ages can be assisted to eliminate their vulnerability in the labor market.

Migrant workers, literally called "farmers-turned-workers" in Chinese, originate from surplus labor in rural areas. It does not necessarily mean that the individuals of this labor force group are unwanted for agricultural production. Contrarily, it is those who better meet the conditions of cross-regional migration that move out of the countryside first. That is, compared to their counterparts left behind in villages, migrants hold some advantageous properties in demographic factors. First, their education attainments are comparatively formal — namely, clustered between the ages of 20 and 30 years, they mostly finished their compulsory education (junior high schooling), which fits unskilled or semi-skilled job requirements. Second, their labor participation rate is high, because they can hardly afford unemployment given the lack of access to social security and employment assistance in urban areas, so they tend to accept lower reservation wages and poorer working conditions. Third, as the source of labor supply, they are segmented to a certain extent from market demand, owing to factors such as spatial distance, institutional exclusion, and information asymmetry.

As a result, agricultural production changes in response to the massive and unremitting outflow of laborers, and the rigid demand of urban sectors for migrant laborers. Therefore, agriculture no longer serves as a pool of surplus labor whenever urban sectors need them in the face of economic downturn. Therefore, this labor group virtually becomes the main force, instead of the reserve, for the urban labor market. Given their status of being less protected by labor market institutions and social security, they are more likely to become a victim of volatile labor market situations caused by macroeconomic fluctuation. Migrant workers' suffering from cyclical unemployment and migrant workers' shortages alternately occurs as the macroeconomy passes in and out of the boom-and-bust cycle.

The unemployment and employment difficulties facing university graduates are new phenomena. Before the mass expansion of university enrollment, university graduates were scarce human resources and thus were an unusually privileged group in the labor market. Despite the fact that the traditional pattern of job planning distribution had already been broken in the 1990s, there were no notable employment difficulties facing them at the time. Employment difficulties became widespread only when the first passel of expanded graduates entered the labor market. In 2001, when the expanded university students had not yet graduated, the share of new graduates who sought jobs through publicly run employment service organizations was 16.5%. In 2002, when the first expanded group of junior college graduates with three years of schooling entered the labor market, that share increased to 20.1%. And in 2009, it further increased to 22.7%, of which 41.5% were that year's university graduates. The estimates, based on one per thousand population sampling survey conducted nationally in 2005, show that the surveyed unemployment rate of junior college graduates was 8%, and that of university graduates was 6.1% — both significantly higher than the urban average of 5.2% (Cai and Wang, 2009, p. 29; Wang and Cai, 2009, p. 57).

While the higher unemployment rate and employment difficulties facing university graduates are no doubt influenced by macroeconomic cycles of boom-and-bust, they are mainly guided by factors of frictional and structural unemployment. In terms of endowments of human capital, university graduates are generally more advantageous than other labor groups, including migrant workers, urban employees, and new entrants with lower education attainments, and therefore they are more likely to work in formal sectors and get a better and more secure pay. However, since their revealed advantage in the labor market is comprehensive knowledge and specific skills, whether such human capital is sufficient to meet the criteria and requirements of the labor market, or moreover, whether their individual expectation matches the labor market, determine the results of their job searching and unemployment risks they face.

The urban laborers with a deficiency of human capital, typically characterized by older ages, low education attainments, poor health, and outdated skills, are another group exposed to natural unemployment shocks. Take education as an example. Based on a study (Wang and Niu, 2009b), in the range of ages between 24 and 64, each additional age of one year reduces the years of schooling by 10.2%. Such a negatively marginal effect becomes more significant at older ages — in the range of 44 to 64, every additional age of one year reduces the years of schooling by 16.1%. Suppose there is a critical minimum level of human capital — presumably, nine years of schooling, the official requirement of compulsory education, the critical age distinguishing between the two groups below and above the criteria is 33 years old.

This group of laborers not only experienced the shocks of unemployment and layoffs during the urban employment policy adjustment aimed at breaking the "iron rice bowl," but they will also face frictional and structural difficulties in employment and reemployment before they reach official retirement age. Holding urban *hukou* and living in urban communities, they can be well covered by formal statistics in terms of their labor market status, in contrast to migrant workers. Their full inclusion and large share in urban registered unemployment, to a certain extent, characterize this indicator. That is, on one hand, the registered unemployed in urban areas has been insensitive to a fluctuating macroeconomy, because the difficulties those laborers face are long-standing and persistent. On the other hand, they are relatively well assisted and protected by various government programs once the indicator identifies them.

Demand for and supply of labor market institutions

The well-functioning labor market is not only reliant on market forces but is also regulated by labor market institutions and complemented by social protection mechanisms. The changed balance between demand for and supply of labor after the Lewis turning point arrival brings about a different demand for and provision of labor market institutions as well. Based on the foregoing analysis on status quo and properties of the three groups — namely, of migrant workers, university graduates, and the vulnerable urban workers at the ongoing Lewis turning point, in what follows, we explore differentiated demand for institutions, reveal the maturity of conditions for providing relevant institutions and bring forward the urgent tasks of labor market development and institutional building in the post-Lewis turning point era.

Given that migrant workers steadily become a major source of the labor force and that they are subjected to cyclical fluctuation in the labor market, there emerges an urgent need to include them into the full coverage of labor market regulations and social protection. The migrant workers' lack of protection in the labor market and poor labor relations are manifested in a small fraction of signing labor contracts, discriminatory pay, wages in arrears, overtime working, and absence of collective bargaining. Furthermore, due to instability of migrants' employment and high contribution rates to various social security programs, there is lack of incentives for both migrant workers and their employers to participate in these programs, giving rise to their low coverage (Table 4.2). Those exclusions of labor market institutions and social protection put them in a position of being exposed to labor market risks and prevent them from serving as the main force of urban labor market stably. Migrant workers' needs thus should be in the center of labor market institutions and social security system building.

Due to the significant differences in human capital endowments and in the demographic characteristics between university graduates and the vulnerable urban workers, the two groups of labor market participants do not seem to share much common ground. However, they are both the congeners most likely to suffer natural unemployment and encounter frictional and structural difficulties in the job market.

Table 4.2. Participation Rates of Migrant Workers in Social Security Programs (%).

	Migrant workers for 6 months and longer	Migrant workers for 1 month and longer
Social pension	9.81	8.72
Injury insurance	24.09	21.93
Medicare insurance	13.1	11.76
Unemployment insurance	3.69	3.28
Reproductive insurance	2.03	1.80
Housing accumulation fund	2.38	2.15

Source: Sheng (2009).

First, both groups seek job trainings in order to adapt to the labor market and to solve structural mismatching between their human capital endowments and skill requirements. Under the circumstances of substantial expansion of enrollment and the serious disjoint of university studies from the needs of the job market, university graduates only have two methods to gain their returns on education. One is to start their first job as unskilled workers and then bridge the skills gap through "learning-by-doing." Another is to first go through a job-oriented training before taking a job with specific skill requirements. The vulnerable urban workers still have the chance to receive training for new skills before retirement. As population aging accelerates and labor shortages become more severe, there will be a stronger demand for this group of laborers. The government has a role to play in the provisions of vocational training for both groups.

Second, the malfunction of the labor market and inadequacy of public employment services are the institutional factors causing frictional unemployment, which urban workers with weak human capital endowment and college graduates, as labor market newcomers, are prone to encounter. After all, since the Chinese labor market development is far from complete, the organizational imperfection in providing job market information, intermediary services, and accommodation of labor supply and demand leads to a larger friction in labor market matching. While the Chinese proactive employment policy has been taking shape in response to the mass lay-offs in the late 1990s and has played an important role in helping the laid-off get reemployed, there are two primary challenges. First, the policy package initiated in tackling the labor market shocks should be upgraded to a normalized mechanism, efficiently dealing with the frictional factors of the labor market. Second, it should be further developed to include the function of aiding university graduates to match their skills and expectations with the needs of the job market.

Third, compared to other labor market participants, the vulnerable urban working group needs more employment assistance and social protection. As a whole, people categorized in this group experienced lay-offs or unemployment during the labor market shocks, and were reemployed in informal jobs, therefore, in most cases, having no formal labor contract and are poorly covered by social security programs. Because they have worked through the two periods — namely, the periods before and after the employment system reform — the deficiency in human capital and resulting employment difficulties facing them are the legacy inherited from the planning system. Before this group exits the labor market, social protection is bound to sufficiently support it.

The ongoing Lewis turning point has been creating incentives compatibility for labor market institutions formation and social protection provision. While observing the changes in the labor market as the result of rapid economic growth and resulting labor shortages in some European countries, Lewis (1979) was impressed to see that labor market institutions, such as collective bargaining, were no longer restricted with fear of overpopulation. This observation implies the impacts of the Lewis turning point on both the demand for and supply of these institutions. Since the government is supposed to be the supplier of labor market institutions and public policies aiming to protect workers' rights in response to the needs of various parties in the labor market, at this turning point, one can expect an essential alteration in policy orientation and government behaviors.

The existing literature mainly focuses on the labor market's reaction to the Lewis turning point — namely, the increased importance of labor relative to physical capital and the resulting enhancement of wages, which leads to changes in employers' behaviors. As a matter of fact, if the government has strong incentives spurring economic development, when they feel the rising pressure of competition from the labor market, they tend to adjust the policy orientation and measures in line with the same direction. In general, China has been conceptualized as a developmental state (Oi, 1999; Walder, 1995), and local governments are seen as competitive governments (Herrmann-Pillath and Feng, 2004). That is, the governments have strong motivation to spur China's economic growth by various policy measures, including legislation, public policy-making, improving the climate of investment and development, helping local businesses to seek financial resources from domestic and foreign investors and subsidies from higher levels of government, intervention in enterprise management, and sometimes running businesses themselves.

The nature of an unlimited labor supply prevented the government from putting laborers first in public policy-making during the time before the Lewis turning point. Or more precisely, they made efforts to promote employment by attracting less capital flows to create jobs. As they recognized the Lewis turning point approaching and labor became a constraint of economic growth, the government began to reorient public policy to care for ordinary workers. The migrant labor shortage first appeared in coastal areas in 2004 and has since become nationwide. In response to this brand new phenomenon and to the central government's scientific outlook on development — namely, "putting the people first," local governments have consciously extended their policy orientation from business-centered to human resources-centered, from focusing on employment opportunities to focusing on job decency, and from protecting locals to including migrants.

While the long-standing dual social structure brought about by a dual economy can hardly be broken up overnight, the Chinese local governments indeed while are becoming more and more motivated by Tiebout-type incentives (Tiebout, 1956) in an attempt to attract human resources by enriching the contents and adjusting the direction of public services. In those areas, where the booming economy continues to raise demand for labor force, a silent reform has been undertaken in the building of labor market institutions and social protection mechanisms. The efforts made by the central and local governments in this arena include the following:

First, the central government actively advances the legislation and law enforcement to regulate the labor market and strengthen social protection. In the year 2008 alone, three labor related laws began being implemented, of which the *Employment Contract Law* emphasizes enhancing employment security and providing better protection for migrant workers and the vulnerable urban workers; the *Employment Promotion Law* clearly claims the responsibility of the government in promoting employment and in eliminating various kinds of labor market discrimination; and the *Labor Disputes Mediation and Arbitration Law* is intended to provide a legal framework for improving labor relations. The Standing Committee of the 11th National People's Congress, the top legislative body, began in 2008, putting the creation and enforcement of laws in social areas at top priority. The *Social Insurance Law*, which aims to guarantee residents' legal rights of inclusion in social insurance programs, is currently being debated among the legislators and is expected to pass in 2010.

Second, in the course of tackling unemployment by implementing proactive employment policies, the governments gradually recognize employment expansion as their top priority. All levels of governments have expanded their financial inputs to build infrastructure of public employment services from national to grassroots levels, and in more and more cases, these services are being extended to cover migrant workers. The government has particularly taken action in response to the changed situation of labor demand and supply and the resulting demand for safeguarding the security of job and pay. One example is the accelerated enhancement in the minimum wage level. In 1998, 14.8% of cities increased their local minimum wages at an average increment of 15.9%. In 2008, the proportion of cities that adjusted their local minimum wages increased to 69.9% at an average increment of 19.4%. Government-supported job training has been undertaken and has widely reached migrant workers and the vulnerable urban working group. In some regions, the governments grant laborers with "training vouchers" to give them choices among different training agencies.

Policy prioritization by Chinese governments can be found in the new expression of macroeconomic policy objectives. Compared to the previous officially announced macroeconomic policy objectives, neither monetary nor fiscal policy explicitly gives priority to employment. The current objectives of macroeconomic policies, however, include: (1) promoting economic growth; (2) expanding employment; (3) stabilizing prices; and (4) retaining balance of international payments, which is an apparent indication of an increased focus on employment in policy priority. The government stimulus investment package, attempting to cope with the financial crisis in 2008 and 2009, indeed manifested this new orientation. According to the distribution plan made by the National Development and Restructuring Commission, the public investment, along with its induced private investment, created 14.6% more jobs, while helping migrant workers transform their employment from manufacturing to the service sector and construction (Cai *et al.*, 2010).

Third, the local governments speed up *hukou* system reform by lowering the threshold for migrants to reside in cities permanently. They are a significant share of the rapidly growing urbanization, which is defined as the share of residents living in cities for more than six months, but many migrant workers still hold agricultural or non-agricultural *hukou*; this can be, to a large extent, attributed to migration from rural to urban areas without changing *hukou* identity (Cai, 2010b). The increase in the share of non-agricultural population has never stagnated and, in fact, it has accelerated when approaching the Lewis turning point. In the period from 1990 to 1999, the share of population with non-agricultural *hukou* increased by 2.3% annually, while the share of urban residents with broader definition increased by 3.1%. In the period from 1999 to 2007, however, the annual growth rate for the share of non-agricultural popula- tion was 3.2%, compared to the growth rate of urban residents at 3.2%. Both the narrowly defined and the broadly defined urbanization have been the fastest in the world (Cai, 2010c).

The rapid increase in the share of non-agricultural population has been attributed to several factors. As a part of *hukou* system reform, criteria for residence in small towns have been greatly lowered since the beginning of the century. Also, the expansion of university enrollment has brought more graduates with rural origin to cities. Third, more medium-sized cit- ies have lowered the criteria to accept migrant workers and their family members. Feeling the pressure of labor shortage, many cities — excluding the largest — began or are preparing to introduce policies to accept more migrants. That is, migrants can become formal residents with local *hukou* if they meet certain criteria, such as purchasing local housing, paying social security contribution for a certain number of years, and having sta- ble labor contract.

Finally, central and local governments have made great efforts to expand the social security coverage of migrant workers. Migrant workers are still left behind in social security coverage, particularly pensions and unemployment insurance. According to the *Employment Contract Law* issued in 2008, and other regulations, migrant workers are entitled to be included in basic urban social security. Although the law has not been perfectly enforced, due partly to the temporary difficulties faced by enter- prises during the financial crisis, intrinsically, the law can still extend the costs of any employer violations and decrease the cost of workers fighting for their rights.

Since there is no legal handicap for migrant workers to participate in various social security programs, the workers' and employers' willing- ness to join rests with the policies' design. Namely, the low portability and high contribution rates set a great barrier for them to participate, given thin profit margins and low wage rates. To enhance the incentives to participate, some municipalities' flexibly lowered the contribution rates of unemployment and injury insurance in accordance with practicality, and effectively expanded their coverage to migrants. As for the pension system, the introduction of the New Rural Pension Program, which calls for a non-contributory portion in order to fully cover all rural residents, provides two opportunities. That is, migrant workers can either join this program in their rural home before they can participate in an urban pension system or benefit from the potential case that this non-contributory social pension is introduced to urban pension schemes. Another effort made by the central government is the promulgation of *Interim Measures on the Transfer of Continuation of Basic Pension for Urban Enterprises Employees*, which stipulates that all workers participate in a basic pension program, where they will be guaranteed transfer of their pension for continuation of both individual and pooling accounts in their new place of work. This new regulation provides an institutionally guaranteed portability for migrant workers' pension entitlement.

Conclusion and Policy Implications

This section provides an analytical framework to characterize the changes in the labor market after the arrival of the Lewis turning point and examined the logic of and nexus among the changes. The Chinese economic development and labor market institutions are not, however, the spontaneous results of the turning point. Instead, the government, as supplier of institutions, is supposed to play a bigger role at that stage. The purpose of this section is to point out that the governments can better tackle the challenges facing the building of labor market institutions and social protection if the specific demands are fully recognized.

As a critical phase of dual economy development, the Lewis turning point usually brings about a host of fundamental changes in the labor market. One of the unique features of the Chinese development of a dual economy is its simultaneity with the transition from planned economy to market economy. Therefore, the arrival of the Lewis turning point in

China has important policy implications, given that it is supposed to reflect the mixed results of both economic development and reform progress, and to produce profound impacts on future trends of economic and social development.

First, the components of labor market participants have changed. Thanks to the removal of institutional barriers to labor mobility between rural and urban areas, as well as across regions, sectors, and enterprises, the hidden unemployment carried over from the planning period, namely rural surplus laborers and urban redundant workers, has been redistributed through the labor market. Due to their different demographic characteristics, migrant workers are subjected to cyclical unemployment, while those in the vulnerable urban working group are more likely to be exposed to natural unemployment. These two labor groups hold a dissimilar status quo, face different challenges, and seek differentiated services from labor market institutions and social protection in their employment.

In addition, university graduates become increasingly important participants of the labor market. In general, they are less vulnerable in the labor market, but they are also subjected to the risk of natural unemployment caused by frictional and structural factors of job matching. Accordingly, it is also necessary to include them in the coverage of labor market institutions and social protection.

Second, the incentives of supplying labor market institutions and social protection have changed. The central and local governments are reaching for their incentives to be compatible in building labor market institutions and social protection mechanism, because all levels of government recognize that strengthening public services in those areas is an inevitable task in order to sustain economic growth and maintain social harmony. The flexibility of government incentives with the demand for institutions claimed by various groups of laborers will motivate more institutional innovations.

Third, the government approach to labor market policy is facing fundamental changes. The changed relationship between the demand for and supply of labor provides a guideline for appropriate confines of functions between government and market and the division of labor between different government departments. The frequently occurring labor shortage by no means implies a mitigation of employment pressure; instead, it requires the government to implement a more comprehensive proactive employment policy package, which involves the Ministry of Finance, the People's Bank of China, and the National Development and Restructuring Commission in tackling cyclical unemployment by means of macroeconomic policies, the Ministry of Human Resources and Social Security and the Ministry of Education in coping with natural unemployment by means of training, job agencies and employment assistance, and the Ministry of Human Resources and Social Security and the Ministry of Civil Affairs in providing better social protection.

Chapter 5

Further Propelling Urbanization and Balanced Regional Development

5.1. Awareness of the "Mezzogiorno Trap" in the Central and Western Regions

"Mezzogiorno" means "the midday sunshine" in Italian and is also the traditional term for southern Italy, which encompasses the southern section of the continental Italian Peninsula and the two major islands of Sicily and Sardinia. In southern Italy, agriculture is the predominant economy. Compared to northern Italy, a wide development gap exists, which draws economists' attention since this scenario is rarely seen in developed countries. Comparably, the development gap between eastern and western Germany could not be narrowed for a long time after the German reunification. Therefore, economists wrote a paper entitled "Two Mezzogiornos," stating that there are two Mezzogiorno cases in Europe. We can find some similarities from the case of long-lasting regional development gaps in these two regions in the developed countries. First of all, the central governments paid great attention to these relatively undeveloped regions and both similarly received a large amount of transfer payment as well as capital investment. Second, the central governments' special care led to the economic growth pattern and industrial structure maladaptive to the resource endowments structure and further led to inadequate employment and inequitable income distribution in these areas. There was a period of economic growth because of the investment factors, which revealed narrower development gaps compared to other regions. However, the economic convergence is not sustainable and will eventually return to the original track. The regional development gaps in southern and northern Italy, as well as eastern and western Germany, still exist. Therefore, we call this phenomenon the "Mezzogiorno trap."

The "trap" in economics is an "equilibrium trap," referring to when an economy stays in a certain development stage (usually an undeveloped stage) for a long time, though external forces can change its original status or initial equilibrium, an internal force can pull it back to the original equilibrium and keep the economy stable and difficult to deviate with any internal or external force in the long term. In fact, economic history reveals that economic development, especially the catch-up of undeveloped economies, does not have such a fated "equilibrium trap." In fact, the economic equilibrium is difficult to deviate because of either institutional restrictions or development strategy drawbacks. The "Mezzogiorno trap" is such a regional development strategy that provides physical resources, but not the human capital and institutional mechanisms for catch-up in the undeveloped regions. That is, it provides external driving forces, but not internal incentive mechanisms for the development, and it promotes the aggregate economic volume growth in the short term with external material input resources, but the industrial structure cannot guarantee the sustainability of the economic growth because it does not apply the economy's comparative advantage.

There are some differences between the two European Mezzogiorno cases that are in such an equilibrium trap. For example, southern Italy faces the dual-sector economic structure transition because its catch-up started from the traditional agricultural economy. Eastern Germany faces more institutional transition challenges, with the key to developing the market economy, because its catch-up started from the planned economy of the former Democratic Republic of Germany. The two undeveloped regions' main tasks are the double transitions that China's central and western regions are facing, i.e., the dual economy structure transition and the transition from planned economy to market economy. Therefore, lessons in the development of the two Mezzogiornos are important references for implementing the catch-up strategy in China's central and western regions.

In the 21st century, the central government has implemented many regional strategies that promote development in the central and western regions, such as the "Western Development" strategy, the "Northeast Old

Industrial Base Revitalization" strategy, and the "Rise of Central China" strategy. In the implementation of these strategies, through many projects, including infrastructure constructions, production capacity construction investment, and subsidies to social security and public services, the central government provided a large amount of capital investment, transfer payment, and other fiscal supports to the central and western regions and largely changed the regional distribution of physical inputs. For example, the share of total investment in fixed assets in the central and western regions increased from 41.2% to 48.1% of the nation's total investment from 2000 to 2008. If we look at the state-owned sector, the share of total investment in fixed assets in the central and western regions increased from 47.0% to 58.2%, which effectively promoted the economic growth and social development in the central and western regions and its economic convergence to the east regions.

Using 2003 as the turning point, the provincial GDP per capita GINI coefficients steadily increased from 1998 to 2003, unweighted GDP per capita GINI coefficient increased from 0.319 in 1998 to 0.341 in 2003, and the corresponding population-weighted GDP per capita GINI coefficient increased from 0.255 to 0.283, both of which reached maximum in 2003. Since then, unweighted GDP per capita GINI coefficient decreased from 0.341 in 2003 to 0.305 in 2007 and the corresponding population-weighted GDP per capita GINI coefficient decreased from 0.283 to 0.265. Such trend had never occurred since the 1990s and it undoubtedly reflects the effects of implementing the regional development strategies.

Does this mean that everything is successful when the economy in the central and western regions converges to the economy in the coastal areas? With the previous lessons of the two Mezzogiornos, we should be concerned about the sustainability of the catch-up in China's central and western regions. It should not be an unnecessary worry that there will be a Chinese type "Mezzogiorno" — that is, unsustainability of the regional catch-up. We should take early caution before it may be too late to correct it. To be more specific, we have observed some problems that will definitely affect the sustainable economic growth in the central and western regions from its current high-speed economic growth.

The first observed phenomenon is that the labor migration still follows the long-term pattern, moving from the central and western regions to the coastal areas, the opposite direction as the manufacturing industry development center moves from the coastal areas to the central and western regions. During 2000 and 2003, the annual growth rate of industrial value added in the east regions was 20.8%, higher than the 13.3% and 15.3% growth rates in the middle regions and the west regions, respectively. However, the situation significantly changed during 2003 and 2007, when the annual growth rate of industrial value added in the east regions raised to 23.6%, but was exceeded by the 24.1% and 26.3% growth rates in the central regions and the west regions, respectively. Many sources show that the labor migration pattern does not change as the industry distribution pattern changes. This inconsistency reveals that the rise of the central and western regions was not driven by labor-intensive industries.

The following observations confirm this conjecture: The capital intensity (using capital labor ratio as the specific indicator) of the manufacturing industry in the central and western regions rapidly rose after 2000, at a rate much faster than that in the coastal areas and its absolute capital intensity level higher than that in the coastal areas after the rapid rise in 2003 and 2004. In other words, manufacturing industries in the central and western regions have been more capital-intensive and heavy industrialized. In the meantime, the wage rate of manufacturing industries in the central and western regions increased too quickly, and the wage growth rates in the central regions and the west regions were 24.9% and 13.5% higher than that in the east regions, respectively. Is this the normal trend? Will it have a positive effect on the sustainable economic growth in the central and western regions? My answer is no.

In 2008, the average GDP per capita in the west, central, and east regions were 15,951 Yuan, 18,542 Yuan, and 36,542 Yuan, respectively, which means that the average income per capita in the west and central regions were only 44% and 51% of that in the east regions, i.e., income differentials were still significant. The development gap, which is defined with income per capita, implies that the difference in resources endowments remain unchanged. That is, developed regions have relatively abundant capital factors and the comparative advantage in capital-intensive industries, while undeveloped regions have abundant labor and the comparative advantage of lower labor cost. Until recently, the conclusion above was still valid, with the fact that a large amount of rural labor was still migrating from the central and western regions to the coastal areas. It implied that the resource endowments structure difference between the east, central, and west regions should have become the economic catch-up opportunity in the central and western regions, which has not come true so far.

With increasing labor costs in the east regions, the comparative advantage in labor-intensive industries in these areas is diminishing. According to the prediction with the conventional "flying-geese" model, labor-intensive industries would gradually migrate to countries with lower labor costs, and, in fact, there is a trend in recent years that reveals new direct foreign investments are flowing to countries such as India, Vietnam, and Cambodia. This change in investment flow is not surprising, however, a more rational "flying-geese" model should be a "domestic version" instead of an "international version." Specifically, the central and western regions should apply its own resource endowments to extend the comparative advantage in labor-intensive industries because of China's vast territory and the diverse resource endowments and different development stages of China's varying regions. So far, China's central and western regions have not chosen the proper route to develop labor-intensive industries. Instead, industries in the central and western regions are becoming more capital-intensive, because the acceleration of industrialization has government-driven and investment-driven characteristics. If China wants to draw lessons from other countries to avoid the "Mezzogiorno trap" in the central and western regions, it should immediately adjust the regional development strategy and pull the development in the central and western regions back to the path with the comparative advantage.

Policy approaches to improve income distribution

Dealing with problems of "growing old before becoming rich" and "growing big before becoming rich" relies on China keeping the sustainable economic growth, raising the income per capita level, and accelerating the transition from a middle-income country to a high-income country. However, simply raising the income per capita level without a suitable income distribution pattern is not enough. Therefore, it is of primary importance for China to improve income distribution and narrow income differentials. In 2009, the central economic working conference raised "to make greater efforts to adjust the national income distribution and develop residents', especially the low-income group's, consumption capability." Improving income distribution involves improving workers' remuneration in the primary distribution of the national income. In fact, with the arrival of the Lewis turning point, improving income distribution is the most urgent task and has a more favorable condition that average workers' income will significantly increase in the new development period. Therefore, increasing the share of workers' remuneration in the primary distribution relies on the continual growth of employment. With the significantly improved relationship of labor supply and labor demand, employment opportunity increases, providing conditions to raise the overall wage level. In fact, with more sufficient rural labor migration and the emergence of labor shortage, average workers' income will gradually increase according to the law of the labor market, which is a reasonable phenomenon and also China's reality in the past few years.

The labor market reacts to changes in the labor supply and demand relationship with its own adjustment mechanism, while the government can make efforts to raise workers' wages and the share of their remuneration in the primary distribution beyond the market force. To facilitate this outcome, the government should make greater efforts to maintain fair competition in the labor market; clear entry barriers of employment opportunities; eliminate sector and enterprise monopoly; prevent labor market discrimination, avoid non-competitive factors' effects on residents' incomes and the wage differences caused by non-human capital factors; further reduce barriers for labor migration between rural and urban areas, sectors, and enterprises through reforming the household registration system and canceling the link between public services and the household registration system; and prevent violations of labor legislation and infringement of workers' rights.

The government should also provide appropriate protections for the labor market using, for example, the minimum wage system. In recent years, local governments raised the minimum wage standard, which has become an important key to regulating the average workers' wages. China temporarily suspended the minimum wage adjustment in 2009 in order to handle the financial crisis and to promote employment and reemployment.

With the improvement of the employment situation and the emergence of the new "peasant worker shortage," provinces began a new round of adjustments in 2010. It is worth noting that in determining the minimum wage standard, the market equilibrium level should be used as a reference. Enterprises' hiring enthusiasm will be hurt beyond this benchmark.

The government's construction of the labor market institutions, especially the tri-party consultation mechanism and the collective wage bargaining system, is in favor of increasing wages and protecting workers. After approaching the turning point of labor supply and demand, the labor market institutions should play an increasing role in wage determination. The practice of influencing the labor market through institutional construction is in favor of resolving contradictions in labor relations and can avoid excessive interventions to the labor market because it is the tri-party (workers, enterprises, and the government) consultation result, which is worth using for reference and should speed up its implementation.

Appropriate redistribution can not only correct and adjust the primary distribution but also significantly improve the primary distribution. Improving the national income redistribution mechanism consists of two aspects: the taxation system reform and equal public service expansion. Appropriate reform of the taxation system should follow the social justice principle. The government can, and should, make a difference in areas that provide all residents with equal access to public services, including social security, compulsory education, and the construction and supply of other social infrastructures. The sufficient supply and coverage of these services will not only replace some personal expenses, produce the income effect that increase residents' income and further improve income distribution, but also eliminate workers and low-income families' fears of unexpected shocks, increase their confidence of consumption.

5.2. Facts and Models about the Urbanization of Peasant Workers

In the following 20 years, the result of China's demographic transition will further reveal that the working-age population will stop growing around 2013 and the total population will reach its maximum before 2030. For a country that has realized high-speed economic growth relying on abundant and inexpensive labor for a long time, dealing with the challenges brought by these transitions, exploiting the potential of demographic dividends, and realizing the transition of the development pattern are the keys to continuing sustainable growth. Discussing the disappearance of China's dual economy from the view of the Lewis turning point and revealing its policy implications can help us to understand the trend of changes in peasant workers' status and identification, reveal the potential of the future economic growth, and maintain a harmonious society.

Two facts about peasant workers

Before approaching the Lewis turning point, labor migration had no negative impact on agricultural production, for there was rural surplus labor, and marginal product of labor was fairly low in agriculture; therefore, for a long time, the migration of peasants did not change the agricultural production pattern. In addition, non-agriculture industries only marginally and unstably absorbed rural surplus labor in the same period of time; agriculture served as a reservoir of surplus labor. After reaching the Lewis turning point, the situation fundamentally changed.

First, the agricultural production pattern has been adjusted in response to the constant and permanent large-scale labor migration, which steers the agriculture technical change to be labor-saving oriented. Comparing the period between 1978 and 1998 with the period between 1998 and 2008, the annual growth rate of large and medium farm tractor gross power increased from 2.0% to 12.2% and the annual growth rate of small farm tractor gross power decreased from 11.3% to 5.2%. The changes in farm tractor tools were similar. According to the induced technological innovation theory, the acceleration of the agricultural mechanization and the labor saving trend prove the substantial reduction of agricultural surplus labor.

Second, urban non-agricultural industries rely more on peasant workers and their demand for peasant workers increasingly becomes rigid. The net urban labor increment almost all comes from rural areas. According to the National Statistics Bureau's investigation, there were 225 million peasant workers who had migrated for non-agricultural work for more than six months by the end of 2008. 140 million peasant workers, which were

62.3% of all peasant workers, migrated across regions. 85 million peasant workers, which were 37.7% of all peasant workers, worked in non-agricultural industries within their home regions. 28.59 million peasant workers, which were 12.7% of the total peasant worker population, migrated their whole families. Before approaching the Lewis turning point, cyclical changes of labor demand in urban or non-agricultural industries usually cause the quantity of agricultural labor to change in the opposite direction. At the time, agricultural employment scale was not determined by its own demand and agriculture was the reservoir of surplus labor. When reaching the turning point, fluctuations in urban and non-agricultural labor demand no longer cause opposite changes in the quantity of agricultural labor, which means that agriculture is no longer the reservoir of surplus labor. China's rapid adjustment on the employment of peasant workers after the financial crisis was evidence of the fundamental changes in the labor market.

The end of the "Todaro dogma"

The economist Michael Todaro thought that the migration decision was based on expected income differentials (adjusted for urban unemployment rate) between urban and rural areas. It is a paradox that all efforts to improve the migrants' situation will cause them to rush into urban areas and aggravate the urban employment and living environment. Therefore the "Todaro paradox" in theory turns into the "Todaro dogma" in policy. For example, assuming that agriculture is still the reservoir of surplus labor, conventional policy efforts are made to keep the balance of pushing forces and pulling forces of migration between rural and urban areas so that the rural areas can play a role to resolve social risks. In so doing, a series of policies is formed in favor of restricting rural–urban migration and treating migrants as temporary guest workers. As long as agriculture does not serve as the reservoir of surplus labor, labor migration will not function as "come and go" pattern, such a dogma will lose the basis for existence. That is, the conventional policies of controlling labor migration based on the "Todaro dogma" is definitely outdated.

Investigations suggest that about 70% of peasant workers have lived in cities for more than three years and 39% of them have lived in cities for over eight years. Although they were counted in the urban population statistically and they contributed to the population urbanization rate of 45% in 2007, many of them do not have a permanent urban residence certificate, i.e., the non-agricultural population rate is only 33% according to the household registration statistics (See Figure 5.1). The differential between the two rates implies that most peasant workers do not receive equal public service or social protection; they bear the brunt in times of crisis, have unstable employment and income as well as low social security coverage, and are the marginal and vulnerable group in the city.

The statistical results show that urban-resident peasant workers and their families do not receive the same social security coverage as permanent registered urban residents and do not receive equal rights in compulsory education, affordable housing, and other public services. The atypical and unstable urbanization deters the function of cities, does not promote the service industry development or the consumption demand expansion, and inhibits the effect of urbanization on economic and social development. Therefore, future urbanization should change direction from simply increasing population rates to concentrating more on the scope and content of the public service coverage expansion, and realize the urbanization of peasant workers through eliminating the household registration system.

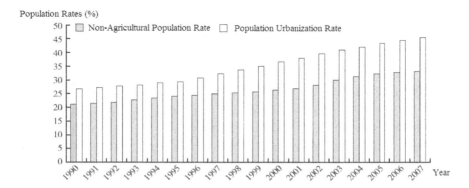

Figure 5.1. Population Urbanization Rate and Non-Agricultural Population Rate.

Source: National Statistics Bureau "Statistical Yearbook of Population and Employment in China" (all previous years), China Statistics Press.

"Tiebout incentive" and public service inclusion

As a development state or competitive government with incentives created by fiscal decentralization, local Chinese governments have a strong motivation to develop the local economy and try to effectively maximize government economic function, including directly intervening in economic activities and providing public goods as long as it is in favor of local economic development. However, such an orientation of government function is changing as a result of the arrival of the Lewis turning point. By constructing a model that migrants "vote with their feet," the economist Charles Tiebout pointed out that local governments can attract or exclude migrants by adjusting their own acts of public service provision if they have specific requirements and preferences on the number of local residents.

With unlimited labor supply, labor would not become the bottleneck for the development of non-agricultural industries. Therefore, the local governments' main areas of intervention are not in the labor market, but in focusing on attracting capital investment. When reaching the Lewis turning point, labor shortages frequently occur, enterprises start competition for labor by paying higher wages and improving working conditions, and local governments involved in the labor market raise the levels of public service to peasant workers and help achieve a better local labor supply environment. The policy responses are mainly reflected in the following aspects.

First, there is greater focus on legislation and law enforcement to protect workers. New legislation significantly regulates enterprises' employment behaviors and improves the labor market institutions. In recent years, labor dispute cases related to peasant workers significantly increase. The number of cases endogenously increases because the enactment and publicity of labor laws cause workers to feel that there are laws to abide by, and in addition, the changes in labor supply and demand relationship, as well as the government's concern for social harmony, make the arbitration and judgments of labor dispute cases more biased to the workers.

Second, the labor market institutions have enhanced roles. A typical change is the raised adjustment frequency and amplitude to the minimum wage standard. The characteristics of the institutions' initial implementation are low standards, low adjustment frequency, and less applicability to peasant workers. After the widespread "peasant worker shortages" in 2004, the central government required local governments to adjust at least once every other year and apply this scheme to peasant workers. Feeling the pressure of labor shortages, local governments frequently increased the minimum wage standards.

Third, there is the enhancement of social security coverage. To raise peasant workers' enthusiasm to participate in insurances, the central government has announced the continuation and transfer approaches of the basic old-age pension insurance to peasant workers. The initiatives of local governments to provide better social protections are more prominent. There are four reflections of this situation: that (1) local governments' spending on basic old-age pension insurance has exceeded the central government; (2) local governments made use of the central easing policy during the financial crisis, consciously lowered peasant workers' payment, and expanded the coverage; (3) local governments promote the improvement of the compulsory education for peasant workers' children; and (4) local governments have enhanced their roles and changed their orientations in helping peasant workers claim delayed wages, arbitrating labor disputes, equal treatment, and other aspects.

Lastly, reform of the household registration system, whose function is to deter labor migration and provide unequal public services, has accelerated. From this point of view, large-scale labor migration has shown progress in the reform of the household registration system. In addition, feeling the pressure of labor shortages, local governments continually lower the home-settling conditions for peasant workers. Even using the narrowly defined urbanization, i.e., the non-agricultural population share, one can see that the speed of China' urbanization is also extraordinary.

Has the institutional condition for the urbanization of peasant workers matured?

Utilizing the "Tiebout incentive" brought by the Lewis turning point, an effective way to promote urbanization is to provide a more stable security and protection system for peasant workers through labor market institutions construction. This will be done by gradually promoting the institutional construction to a wider range of public service aspects, realizing the true meaning of urbanization, and through urbanization and non-agriculturization synchronization.

However, not every institutional condition for promoting the urbanization of peasant workers is prepared. After the tax-sharing reform in 1994, China formed the asymmetric relations of fiscal capacity and administrative responsibilities between central and local governments. Although development-oriented local governments have a greater incentive to improve public services for peasant workers and substantially promote the reform of the household registration system, the current tax system will put them into a tight situation. Therefore, increasing local governments' revenue proportions through tax system reforms and making the fiscal capacity and administrative responsibilities more symmetric is the key to promoting in-depth urbanization and steering the reform of government function in the right direction.

5.3. A Tale of Two Cities: Diversity in the Household Registration System Reform

Since the 21st century, many Chinese cities have announced and piloted the household registration system reforms and, despite mixed results, the locally-driven and local decision-making may well characterize such reforms. Because the household registration system, an institutional arrangement of the dual economy with Chinese characteristics, is the mutual target of the reforms, the practices have general characteristics, which can be summarized as the equal provision of public services and the conditional access for migrant workers to local registration. However, observing the specific local practices and effects, one can find that most reforms did not have a dramatic breakthrough, either because the threshold for entry was still too high for peasant workers, or migrant peasants did not enjoy equal public services even after nominally becoming registered urban residents.

In terms of approach to promoting the reform, the new round of household registration system reforms in Chongqing and Chengdu, two municipalities that were assigned by the central government as pilot zones of integrating the rural and urban developments, meet the two criteria of reform — namely, equal provisions of public services between rural and urban areas and lowered entry barriers for migrant workers to settle in cities. For example, the requirements for migrant workers' time length of working in cities, housing purchase, and investment criteria and tax amount became much more attainable, and migrant households may fully enjoy the same employment opportunities and assistance, social security programs, subsidized housing, education and medical treatment as permanent residents once they are granted with identity of urban residents. Therefore, the reform deserves high recognition and warm welcome.

Without alteration of household registration, migrant workers, even when they live in cities for a long time, cannot receive equal public services, lack secure jobs, and do not change consumption patterns, therefore, the new reform in the household registration system has substantial significance.

In a previous paper, I predicted that local governments would have a greater incentive to promote the household registration system reform when China enters a new economic development period, i.e., after reaching the Lewis turning point. Generally speaking, because labor gradually becomes a scarce factor, local governments have the similar incentive to attract and keep migrant workers, like their previous efforts in attracting investments, resulting in the launch of a series of related reforms, including the household registration system reform. However, different regions face different situations and have different reform incentives. So far, the reform incentive in Chongqing and Chengdu is not to solve the labor shortage problem, because the western regions still have a relative abundance of laborers under a significant dual economic structure. In fact, is the two cities are facing the development problem in capital and land (which is synonymous with capital). As a result, non-agricultural land has become the restricting factor for their further development. The central government should recognize and allow such an incentive in obtaining land to promote the household registration system reform in those regions like Chongqing and Chengdu.

The household registration system reform in Chongqing and Chengdu has a clear feature of institutions designs, which is especially reflected in the planning of migrant peasants' land usage. The reform initiation in

Chongqing and Chengdu is designed to properly relocate the plots of land vacated by urbanized rural families. According to the policies issued by the local governments, the land relocation includes three steps. First, local governments compensate for the plots of contracted arable land and house sites based on land expropriation regulations and referring to the current price of land voucher. Then the returned house sites are required to reclaim their original localities, their land use quota is traded within the municipalities, and the quota may be used as construction land in other localities of the municipalities. Next, the claiming right of the land is held for the transferred households for three years in case they return for reasons such as employment shock. The unified utilization of the quota of land vacated by official migration from rural to urban areas is the motivation of Chongqing and Chengdu municipal governments implementing the household registration system reform.

Institutional reforms need motivations and governments themselves should have incentives in the household registration system, which involves government's actions. Attempting to promote the reform of the household registration system without recognition of the governments' reforming incentive is somewhat utopian and naive.

For whatever motivation, the household registration system reforms in Chongqing and Chengdu meet the government's goal to obtain non-agricultural land for urbanization, while they serve the overall objectives of the country as a whole. First of all, the reform transforms tens of millions of peasants into urban residents within 10 years, helping them to obtain more non-agricultural employment opportunities, enjoying better basic and extended public services, and more sufficiently share the benefits of economic growth and social development. Second, through raising the social security coverage rate and average families' income levels, it is expected to realize the original intention of the reform, which is to correspondingly change the new urban residents' consumption pattern, and provide more demand for urban infrastructure construction, housing construction, and consumption commodities productions.

Therefore, we can find that the household registration system reform in Chongqing and Chengdu is in favor of addressing the major challenges that China faces, i.e., through the urbanization of peasants and peasant workers, expanding domestic consumption demand, exploiting demographic dividends, exploring sustainable economic growth, and enhancing the coordination between the economic growth and social development after approaching the Lewis turning point. In addition, we should look into the unclear aspects of the household registration system reform in Chongqing and Chengdu. In other words, we should address the unsolved questions of the reform so far and further raise some policy suggestions.

First of all, the main beneficiaries in the household registration system reform in Chongqing and Chengdu are registered permanent resident peasants within the two jurisdictions, and the reform has not yet benefited peasant workers who migrate from other administrative areas. Chongqing and Chengdu are not areas typical of influx of migrant peasant workers from other provinces. Therefore, it is acceptable that the reform is currently restricted to local residents. However, for the general cases in China, the household registration system reforms should seek to realize the urbanization of peasant workers and their families who migrate across provinces. China has about 145 million peasant workers who migrate across regions, and at least tens of millions of family dependents migrating with them; above 95% of migrant peasant workers reside and work in urban areas, above 80% of them are located in cities, and 51% of them migrate across provinces. Therefore, if the entire country follows Chongqing's and Chengdu's reform pattern (e.g., famous household registration system pilot in Guangdong province is also restricted to the peasant workers registered in the province), it implies that the peasant workers who migrate from the central and western regions to the coastal areas will be left out by the household registration system reform and the people-centered urbanization is still in an indefinite future.

Second, Chongqing and Chengdu allow migrant peasants to keep their rights to use their contracted land and residence land for certain years. Although the provision leaves ground for a retreat, is it more flexible and humane to allow migrant peasants to decide when to exit the land? In Japan, during the 1960s, when peasants massively rushed into cities, the Japanese government did not force the migrant peasants to sell their land. In fact, their land ownerships are even retained to this day. Japan's experience is, on one hand, keeping the land ownership system to dissolve migrant workers' worries; but on the other hand, experience has shown that, with the arrival of the Lewis turning point, urban labor demand continually expands and, with the modernization of agricultural production, agriculture is no longer the reservoir of surplus labor and migrant peasants will not move back to rural areas.

Our research shows that China is currently at a similar stage of economic development as Japan in the early 1960s, where it is irreversible for rural labor to migrate and settle down in urban areas. Therefore, the market mechanism that helps the mobility of contracted land and residence land in rural areas can better compensate outflow farmers, protect the interests of peasants, and transform the means of agricultural production into the seed funding for migrant workers' production and lives in urban areas.

Lastly, whether the unique land quota trading system in Chongqing and Chengdu can eventually achieve success and recognition depends on the reclamation of the replaced land. Beyond the scope of the two cities, this relates to the overall reservation of arable land of the country as a whole. In the new rural construction campaign, there are many discussions about merging villages and collectively constructing buildings in order to replace the original village sites and residence land for reclaiming, but many examples, in reality, show that the reclaiming does not occur. Local governments need incentives to promote the household registration system reform and they also need the legitimacy, i.e., keeping the baseline of developing land. Therefore, through designing the incentive and punishment mechanism, the success of the reform depends on the reasonable and lawful land utilization.

After all, governments can promote household registration system reforms with different motivations. For example, attracting and keeping human resource in the coastal areas, exploiting the potential of domestic demand in the central and western regions, and breaking the resource (land) bottleneck for economic development in areas that urgently need to catch up. Different incentives will form different mechanism designs and promotion methods and further form diversity in the household registration system reform. Therefore, diversity is the must-follow path for decentralized reforms and its advantage. Allowing the diversity of reforms is the key to ensuring that there is incentive, driving force, and a greater chance of success for the reforms.

5.4. Extended Reading: The *Hukou* Reform and Unification of Rural-Urban Social Welfare

Introduction

The professed function of the Chinese household registration (or *hukou*) system, formed in the late 1950s, is to separately register population in rural and urban areas. Distinguishing the rural or urban birthplace determines the legitimate residence of any Chinese citizen, which is identified by the *hukou*. To transfer household registration from rural to urban areas is conditional, and the criteria for such transfer are terribly strict, constraining the rights of free migration for rural residents. *Hukou* was implemented, typically and strictly, before and during the early period of Chinese reform. While it is commonly believed that, in the past 30 years, overall economic reform has been accompanied by the reform of the *hukou* system to some extent, the actual development of the *hukou* system has not been recognized fully or properly valued by academia (e.g., Chan and Buckingham, 2008; Chan, 2010). In a more extreme case (Whyte, 2010), *hukou*-related rural–urban divide has been compared to the India-type caste system. Such an underrating of the progress of reform in this area originates from a narrow understanding of the *hukou* system. That is, if the *hukou* system is merely viewed as a population-registration system distinguishing rural and urban residents, no significant change can be perceived.

However, when scholars advocate *hukou* reform and both central and local governments actually conduct various reform experiments, their efforts are not confined to only eliminating the regional separation of population. To understand the essential meaning of the *hukou* system, one must explore the primary motive for its initiation, as well as its resultant characteristics (e.g., see Cai, 2010a). *Hukou* was first introduced to serve as an invisible wall to prevent the rural labor force from moving out of agriculture; thus, it is closely linked to an exclusive employment system in urban sectors. Second, it was adopted to guarantee basic living and minimum social welfare for urban residents, and therefore, it ought to develop an institutional arrangement in order to separate *hukou* residents' entitlements from those of migrants. In taking into account the wider functions of the *hukou* system — instead of viewing it only as population registration — it should be clear that, as the Chinese economy transitions to a market economy, the *hukou* reform should not only progress simultaneously, but also should be carried out on a much wider scope.

As in the other areas of Chinese economic reform, *hukou* reform has been carried out in both bottom-up and top-down ways. On one hand, in seeking higher income and improved standards of living, rural laborers have migrated beyond the resident and employment boundaries set by *hukou* during the reform period. On the other hand, as the reallocation efficiency generated by labor mobility among sectors has become apparent,[1] Chinese governments at various levels first acquiesced to rural laborers' departures from farms and villages and have gradually altered policies over time to actually encourage farmers to leave their rural residences by actively improving the conditions for workers who have moved to cities. Since *hukou* reform involves the alteration and abolition of a series of longstanding institutions, the governments' incentives and initiatives are particularly important in the process. Documenting and explaining such reforms requires exploring motives, behaviors, and the interactions of all participants — namely, rural laborers, urban residents, and central and local governments — under an analytical framework of political economy.

The Chinese economy has been undertaking double transitions: a transition from a dual economy to a more integrated economy and a transition from a planning economy to a market economy. The two transitions have imbued *hukou* reform with important characteristics and divided it into three phases. In its first phase, roughly between the early 1980s and mid-1990s, the reform was marginally carried out under the constraints of a planning economy. Spurred by the clearer market orientation of the overall reform laid out by the Chinese leadership, reform accelerated in the period between the mid-1990s and the early 21st century, say 2003. As the Chinese dual economy entered a new stage after 2003, a year of significance for the Chinese economy, the reform entered its more pivotal period. While in each of the

---

[1] Cai and Wang (1999) estimate that, in addition to the conventional contributions made by physical capital, labor, and education, labor mobility from low productivity agriculture to higher productivity non-agricultural sectors contributed 21% to China's GDP growth in the period from 1978 to 1998. The World Bank (1997) estimated that the contribution of labor mobility to GDP growth was 16%.

phases, the reform of the *hukou* system has made some crucial progresses, the latest round of reform has been much more comprehensive, aimed at completely eliminating the *hukou* system and affiliated institutions.

This section explains the efforts that have been made for reforming the *hukou* system — as government policies respond to changing conditions — by dividing reforms into three phases. Unlike existing literature that focuses more on the unfinished aspects of reform, this paper positively evaluates progress to date and suggests further tasks by revealing the logic of reform, which is closely related to the changing economic stages. This section views *hukou* not only as a population residence regulation, but also as a method for examining changes in the intention and implementation of social welfare programs.

The next part depicts *hukou* reform in the context of the transition from a planned economy to a market economy, which occurred in the course of a typical dual economy development. The following section discusses the arrival of the Lewisian turning point, a new stage of Chinese economic development, and its implications for migrant workers' demands for new institutional settings and the governments' enhanced motives for *hukou* reform. The final section concludes by identifying some dilemmas and proposing policy suggestions for future reform.

Hukou Reform as Institutional Transition

As is commonly known, Chinese economic reform was initiated in rural areas and was characterized by the introduction of the household responsibility system, which, by solving the longstanding incentives problems, undisputedly enhanced the labor productivity of the agriculture sector, freeing up a new surplus of laborers who had accumulated during the pre-reform period. Consequently, Chinese farmers, after earning basic living through their farms, began to seek off-farm work to increase their income. Although economic reform at the time did not aim to relinquish the planning system, *hukou* reform actually took place without a clear blueprint of the overall reform. *Hukou* reform was represented by labor mobility, from agricultural to non-agricultural sectors in rural areas, as well as from villages to nearby towns.

Before the urbanization policy was relaxed to allow rural-to-urban migration, it is widely believed that the labor transfer had long been characterized by local relocation to township and village enterprises (TVEs). It is true that, before the mid-1980s, the central government intended to create a pattern of "leaving the land without leaving the countryside." The development of TVEs, however, was confined to local villages and small towns and was extremely uneven among regions, therefore incapable of creating adequate non-agricultural employment opportunities for the surplus laborers. In 1985, only 18.8% of 370 million rural laborers were engaged in TVEs. According to a scholarly estimation, at the time there were 100–150 million surplus laborers in rural areas, or 30–40% of the total rural workforce (Taylor, 1993, Chapter 8). In order to tackle such a development challenge, farmers sought to break down institutional obstacles and migrated across regional boundaries, while both central and local governments responded to the desires and actions of rural laborers by relaxing institutional constraints for labor mobility.

As reforms in urban areas were initiated in the mid-1980s, and the development of the TVEs stagnated, rural laborers began to migrate across regions, particularly from rural to urban areas in search of non-agricultural jobs. The gradual abolition of institutional obstacles has been key for increased labor mobility since the 1980s. After observing the rural sectors' narrowing capacity for absorbing surplus labor, the government began allowing farmers to engage in long-distance transport and marketing of their products beyond local marketplaces in 1983 — the first time that Chinese farmers had received legitimate rights for doing business outside their hometowns. In 1984, regulations were further relaxed and farmers were encouraged by the state to work in nearby small towns. A major policy reform took place in 1988, when the central government allowed farmers to work in enterprises or run their own businesses in cities, under the condition that they continued to be self-sufficient in terms of staples, in the light of the still-existing rationing scheme. In the 1990s, the central and local governments relaxed policies restricting migration, which also implied a certain degree of reform in the household registration system.

In that period, however, the planning system had not yet been abandoned and the *hukou* system was taken for granted in the institutional setting. That is, any policy adjustment or any action conducted spontaneously by laborers and acquiesced to by the governments was still circumscribed by the strict *hukou* control. In other words, all adjustments and actions outside of the institutional frame were allowed and tolerated only when they fit with certain situations, such as the need for a labor force; when they did not, they were repressed. *Hukou* reform was only marginal and reversible at the time when planning was still in effect.

The official establishment of a market economy as the goal of Chinese reform in the 1990s made the decade a turning point in terms of *hukou* reform. Symbolized by Deng Xiaoping's famous speech tour of South China, as well as the Fourteenth National Congress of the Communist Party of China in the early 1990s, China's reform and opening-up entered a new era. Because of the accelerated *hukou* reform, labor market development, and population migration, the mid-1990s are considered to be the milestone that distinguishes the first and second phases of *hukou* reform.

In this period, the fast growth of labor-intensive and export-oriented sectors, mostly in the coastal provinces, and the dramatic surge of non-public sectors in urban areas, generated a huge incremental demand for labor, spurring a migratory tide of labor that moved from rural to urban sectors and from the central and western to the eastern regions. Conforming to such trends of labor market expansion and integration, a host of reform measures were carried out to eliminate the institutional barriers that deterred labor mobility. For example, the rationing system that was initiated in the mid-1950s to limit supplies of staple foods and other life necessities in cities was abolished in the early 1990s, unlocking one of the most important shackles stopping population migration from rural to urban areas.

Another manifestation of labor market development can be seen in the reform of urban employment policies. Since the mid-1990s, the government granted state-owned enterprises (SOEs) with autonomous powers of hiring and firing employees, which SOE managers took advantage of to break the long-standing "iron rice bowl" (jobs with guaranteed security). During the macroeconomic downturn and East Asian financial crisis, which gave rise to massive layoffs and unemployment in the urban sectors in the late 1990s, the government implemented a layoff subsidy program and built up an unemployment insurance system, a basic pension regime, and a minimum living standard program. While those measures were initiated to protect urban workers, they created an environment for labor market development and liberalized labor market regulations to encourage labor mobility across enterprises, sectors, ownerships, and regions.

In response to the matured economic conditions for labor mobility, in 1998, the Ministry of Public Security gave a green light for the entry of people into cities, such that children could carry out household registration with either parent, couples who had long been separated could be reunited and obtain a change of household registration, the elderly could obtain city *hukou* along with their children, and so on. Although resistance to these reforms was encountered in some major cities, future reform of the household registration system was provided with a legitimate basis at the central government level.

China had been typified by its dual economy development before this phase ended. The rural surplus labor force endlessly migrated to urban sectors in coastal areas, seeking non-agricultural wage employment, and the wage rates of migrant workers remained unchanged and low compared to their urban counterparts, partially because of the nature of the unlimited supply of labor and partially because of the *hukou* system. Despite the expanded labor mobility and a certain progress in reform, the *hukou* system still played two roles, serving its traditional function.

First, the *hukou* system guaranteed the priority of urban laborers for employment opportunities in urban sectors. Due to the coexistence of rural labor surplus and urban workforce redundancy, there existed, to a certain extent, job competition between migrant workers and unskilled urban workers, causing the urban governments to protect local workers and discriminate against migrant workers via *hukou* identification. In an empirical study, Cai *et al.* (2001) found that in this period, urban governments' policies toward inflows of migrants changed cyclically as employment pressures facing local governments changed over time — that is, each time the local unemployment problems became severe, in addition to regular restriction on migrants' employment,[2] they tended to take measures to supplant migrant workers.

---

[2] In the 1990s, some large cities issued policies forbidding urban enterprises from hiring migrant workers for certain jobs that would compete with local workers (Cai *et al.*, 2001).

Second, the *hukou* system excluded migrants from obtaining equal access to urban social welfare services. In the course of tackling the employment shock in the late 1990s, the governments built a preliminary social protection system for urban workers, including programs of basic pension insurance, basic health care insurance, unemployment insurance, and a minimum living standard guarantee plan. Whereas those programs did not provide full coverage for all urban workers, they *officially* included all workers with urban *hukou* and excluded rural-to-urban migrants. In addition, migrant workers were not entitled to public employment assistance programs and thus were exposed to all kinds of employment shocks without formal social protection.

In a dual economy characterized by an unlimited supply of labor, the interests of urban residents typically conflict with that of rural residents, and the urbanites have stronger bargaining power to influence policy-making and thus gain a more advantageous status (Olson, 1985). This was empirically confirmed in the case of *hukou* reform in that period (Cai, 2010c) — that is, when some efforts were made by both central and local governments, they turned out to be futile in the final analysis. Initiated in 2000, *hukou* control of all Chinese small towns was relaxed by significantly lowering the thresholds for residence, while some medium and large-sized cities, including provincial capital cities, such as Shijiazhuang of Hebei province, tried to do the same. Owing to the lack of employment opportunities and capabilities of providing equal social welfare, such as basic pension, health care insurance, access to education, and entrance to higher school for the newcomers, the reform failed to attract many to apply for local *hukou* status. In other cases, where cities abolished the distinction between agricultural and non-agricultural *hukou* identity, due to the remaining unequal social welfare among people living in rural and urban areas, the reform amounted to no more than an insincere promise (Wang and Cai, 2010).

Lewisian Turning Point and Reform Incentives

While the mass labor migration from rural to urban sectors has naturally reduced the degree of labor surplus in agriculture (Cai and Wang, 2008), and the demographic transition in China has reached the stage at which the growth rate of the working-age population is declining (Cai, 2010a), the fast economic growth has continued to generate huge labor demand, leading to demand for labor exceeding supply. Since 2003, the difficulty of hiring migrant workers, and the labor shortage in general, has become widespread and wages of migrant workers have significantly increased year by year. In addition, the wage rates of hired workers in agricultural sectors have also improved (Table 5.1), indicating the shrinkage of surplus labor in agriculture, the shortage of unskilled workers in urban areas, and the ensuing wage increases in all sectors (Wang, 2010).

According to the definition set forth by Lewis (1954), those phenomena indicate that the Chinese economy has arrived at its Lewisian turning point — a period of time in which the wages of ordinary workers increase because labor demand exceeds that of labor supply (Cai and Wang, 2010). At the same time, the *hukou* reform starts its new phase and is expected to make a more fundamental breakthrough. Because 2003 witnessed so many dramatic changes in the Chinese economy and society — e.g., the first labor shortage in China's economic development, the subsequent increase in ordinary workers' wages, the rise of labor cost and fall of labor input in agriculture, and the governments' efforts to improve conditions of migrants living and working in cities in response to those changes (Wang,

Table 5.1.   Increments of Working Age Population and of Employment (Million).

	Working population (1)	Migrant workers (2)	Urban employment (3)	Absorbed hidden unemployment (4)*
2002	15.11	20.71	8.40	−14.00
2003	13.05	9.20	8.59	−4.74
2004	14.70	4.33	8.37	2.00
2005	1436	7.55	8.55	−1.74
2006	8.54	6.34	9.79	−7.59
2007	7.82	4.85	10.40	−7.43
2008	7.54	3.44	8.60	−4.50
2009	6.65	4.59	11.02	−8.96

Note: * (4) = (1) − [(2) + (3)]

Source: Data of working age population is based on estimation by Hu (2009); data on migrant workers is from NBS-DORSES (various years), the 2009 figure is from NDRC (2010).

2010) — it is viewed as a symbolic year, indicating the Lewisian turning point and the outset of a new phase of *hukou* reform.

The essential manifestation of a Lewisian turning point is the alteration of the labor market from an unlimited supply of labor to the frequent emergence of labor shortages. That is, the invariable wage rate can no longer maintain the endless supply of labor, on one hand, and the wage rate increase alone cannot adequately satisfy the workers, who also expect policy reforms in accordance with the changes of development stages. In terms of challenges facing China, this phase of reform can be characterized as follows: First, as the market orientation becomes a clear blueprint of China's overall reform, the *hukou* reform's goal is set to unify the rural and urban labor markets; second, as the unlimited supply of labor is no longer the property of the Chinese economy and the structural factors, rather than magnitude factors, dominate the labor market, the direct conflict in employment between migrant and local workers has been eased; Third, as the social welfare provisions, mainly the social security programs, become pooled based on public finance and individual contribution, there is more compatibility than competition between newcomers and native residents in urban areas. The changes in the reform climate indicate that the governments' intentions and behaviors regarding *hukou* reform are now essentially different from those in the previous phase of reform.

In general, Chinese governments have been conceptualized as a developmental state (Oi, 1999; Walder, 1995), and local governments as competitive governments, in particular (Herrmann-Pillath and Feng, 2004). That is, governments have strong motivation to spur economic growth by various policy measures, including legislation, public policymaking, improving the climate of investment and development, helping local businesses to seek financial resources from domestic and foreign investors and subsidies from higher levels of government, intervention in enterprise management, and sometimes running businesses themselves. As they recognize that the Lewisian turning point is reached and labor becomes a constraint of economic growth, the governments begin to reorient public policy from focusing on employment opportunities to focusing on job decency, and from protecting locals only to including migrants, which leads to institutional changes.

Generally, the developmental state with Chinese characteristics has been undergoing a transformation following its own logic of development stages. That is, the Chinese local governments indeed become more and more motivated by Tiebout-type incentives (Tiebout, 1956) to try to attract human resources by enriching the contents and adjusting the direction of public services. In those areas, where the booming economy continues to raise demand for the labor force, a soundless reform has been undertaken in the building of labor market institutions and social protection mechanisms — incentives compatible with the central government's objective to building a harmonious society (Cai, 2010b).

Such a new policy climate has catalyzed the building of labor market institutions in which migrant workers are now formally included. Symbolized by the satisfactory resolution of the legislative problem predicating the Sun Zhigang incident in 2003[3] and President Hu Jintao's intervention in the wages arrears for migrant workers incident in 2004, labor-related institutions have since evolved in two directions — regulations aiming to protect all workers and deregulations aiming to liberalize labor mobility (Cai, 2010d). In tackling the problems of migrant workers' unsecure employment, poor working conditions, low coverage of social insurance, and lack of protection, governments have made various efforts related to *hukou* system reform.

First, the Employment Contract Law came into effect in 2008. This legislation, which attracted worldwide attention, requires enterprises to sign labor contracts with all employees, regardless of their *hukou* status, and to include them in basic social insurance programs. The Labor Disputes Mediation and Arbitration Law issued the same year encourages migrant workers to initiate labor disputes by cutting litigation costs to almost zero.

Second, local governments have increased the frequency and scale of minimum wage adjustments. During the early years of the implementation

---

[3] A 27-year-old university graduate, Sun Zhigang, was detained by the police and beaten to death because of his lack of a local *hukou* or local temporary resident permit. This attracted widespread public criticism of the *hukou* system and led to the abolition of the State Council regulation, "Approaches to the Custody and Repatriation of Urban Vagrants and Beggars," upon which the criminal acts of the law enforcement officers were based on (see Cai, 2010d).

of this program in the 1990s, the minimum wage standard was low, rarely increased, and hardly applied to migrant workers. As the labor shortage became widespread after 2003, the central government required local governments to adjust the level of minimum wages every other year and to apply the program to migrant workers. Pressured by labor shortage, municipal authorities have since increased the adjustment frequency and local level of the minimum wages.

Third, one of the efforts made by the central government to enhance migrant workers' coverage in basic social insurance programs is the promulgation of Interim Measures on the Transfer of Continuation of Basic Pension for Urban Enterprises Employees in 2010, which stipulates that all workers participating in basic pension programs while migrating across provincial boundaries will be guaranteed a transfer and continuation of both individual and pooling pension accounts in their new places of work. This new regulation provides institutionally guaranteed portability for migrant workers' pension entitlements.

New Wave of *Hukou* Reform

In a paper on *hukou* reform, Cai (2010b) identifies a dilemma that occurs in *hukou* reform — the more social welfare benefits a *hukou* identity contains, the more difficult it is to push forward the reform; but without *hukou* reform, there is no way to detach social welfare benefits from *hukou* status, which has often brought the reform into stalemate. The reorientation of government functions toward public service provision, spurred by the arrival of the Lewisian turning point, along with labor market institution-building, can help break such a dilemma and boost the new round of *hukou* reform. The fundamental change in the policy climate has made the new round of reform more thorough and plausible. Here, we elaborate the practice and progress of the reforms of the *hukou* system and related institutions since 2003.

The number of migrant workers leaving their home townships for six months and longer increased from 114 million in 2003 to 145 million in 2009, of which 95.6% migrated to cities and towns. As Chinese urban residents were statistically defined as those who live in cities for six months and longer when the Fifth National Census was conducted in 2000, the

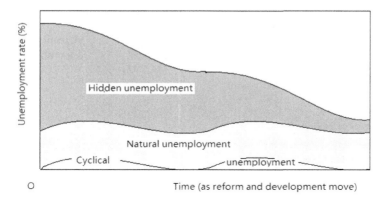

Figure 5.2.   Unemployment Types and Their Changing Trends as Reforms Deepen.

migrant workers and accompanying family members contribute a large part of the increase in number of urban residents during that period. In 2009, the urbanization rate — the share of population living in cities for six months or longer — was 46.6%. Those migrants, however, after moving to cities, do not obtain urban *hukou* status and therefore do not have equal access to social welfare like their counterparts with urban *hukou*. The distinction in social treatment is based on and identified by agricultural *hukou* and non-agricultural *hukou*. In 2007, the share of population with non-agricultural *hukou*, which all native urbanites hold, was 33%, 12 percentage points less than the statistical urbanization rate of the year (Figure 5.2).

Taking account of the difference between the statistical urbanization rate and the non-agricultural rate of population, many scholars and policy researchers assert that the *hukou* reform has not made noticeable progress and the urbanization level has been overestimated (e.g., see Chan, 2010; Chang, 2010). Those arguments are partially correct, because whereas long-term migrant workers are counted as urban residents, they are still excluded from equitable entitlement to many public services provided by urban governments. For example, their participation rates in social insurance programs are significantly lower than those of local workers (Table 5.2), their children have difficulty enrolling in compulsory schooling, let alone entering a higher education school, and they are not entitled to minimum living standard guarantee. As previously noted, however, migrant workers and their accompanying

Table 5.2. Participation Rates of Migrant Workers in Social Security Programs (%)

	Migrant workers for 6 months and longer	**Migrant workers for 1 month and longer**
Social pension	9.81	8.72
Injury insurance	24.09	21.93
Medicare insurance	13.1	11.76
Unemployment insurance	3.69	3.28
Reproductive insurance	2.03	1.80
Housing accumulation fund	2.38	2.15

Source: Sheng (2009).

family members now have much better access to public services than they did previously. Moreover, the *hukou* reform of formally accepting migrants as non-agricultural residents in urban areas has been accelerated.

The share of population with non-agricultural *hukou* has increased since 2003, with faster growth than during the previous period. For example, annual growth rates of the non-agricultural population increased from 3.4% in 1991–2002 to 4.3% in 2002–2007. Given that the natural growth rate of population in both rural and urban China has declined to very low levels — that is, the natural growth of population of the country as a whole decreased from 1.3% in 1991 to 0.5% in 2007 — the increase in the share of non-agricultural population is mainly attributed to mechanical growth, or the rural-to-urban migration with *hukou* change. While the expansion of university enrollment may contribute to the increase, because the rural enrolled students can change their agricultural *hukou* to non-agricultural *hukou* by regulation, the share of students of rural origin in total number of enrolled students declined dramatically in recent years, meaning that the two factors cancel each other out.[4] Therefore, the majority of the new non-agricultural *hukou* population is those who have been officially accepted for migration to destination cities.

As the Chinese economy has recovered from the 2008–2009 financial crisis and then encountered unprecedented labor shortage, many

---

[4] Among the currently enrolled university students, the share of students of rural origin is 17.7%, a big decrease compared to that of more than 30% in the 1980s (Li, 2009).

provinces and cities have initiated a new round of *hukou* reform that is different from the previous reforms in at least two ways.

First, the motive of the new round of reform is endogenous and strong. In terms of the governments' incentives to reform *hukou*, two facts are worth attention: (i) The shortage of migrant workers, beginning in 2003 and becoming increasingly severe after the recovery from the financial crisis in 2010, has caused real difficulty for enterprises in maximizing production capacities throughout the country. In response, for governments in coastal areas, where enterprises suffer difficulty in recruiting workers the most, *hukou* reform has become a policy measure to stabilize labor supply; (ii) Under the strictest control over arable land use, the only method of land exploitation for the local governments who intend to boost urbanization is to reclaim plots of contracted arable land and housing sites that migrated households left behind and to use the quota of those plots elsewhere in order to balance the exploitation and reclamation of land.

Second, the measures taken for the new round of reform are more feasible. Since the beginning of this century, many areas have announced and piloted *hukou* reform. Despite its differing effects from place to place, the reforms have all been initiated locally to conform to the actual needs of the individual localities. Since the objective of the reform is the institutional format of the dual societal structure, the *hukou* system, the reforms share some common features across the areas in which they have been implemented. That is, reform has been bound to equalize public service provisions and pushed by lowering the threshold-of-entry criteria for in-migrants. Neither high thresholds for migrants obtaining a local *hukou* nor segregated treatments of social welfare between newcomers and natives can make the reform successful. As local governments become more aware of the importance of *hukou* reform as an indispensable engine in accelarating urbanization, they tend to substantially ease the criteria for accepting new residents.

While Guangdong, the coastal province of Southern China, initiated *hukou* reform in response to labor shortage in its exports-oriented sectors, the pilot reform in Chongqing, a more agrarian municipality in Southwestern China, is a typical example of a city trying to obtain necessary land for urban expansion. As a less-developed region, Chongqing is bottlenecked more by land than by labor in its efforts to catch up with its more developed counterparts. Since any reform needs to be boosted by incentives and the reform of *hukou* policy that counts on the initiative of government needs to be motivated by governments' will to it, in particular, linking the *hukou* reform with land development is not only the feature but also the motive for the municipality's reform.

The *hukou* reform initiation in Chongqing is designed to properly relocate the plots of land vacated by urbanized rural families. According to the policies issued by the government, the land relocation includes three steps. First, local governments compensate for the plots of contracted arable land and housing sites based on land expropriation regulations and referring to the current price of land voucher.[5] Second, the returned housing sites are required to reclaim their original localities, their land use quota is traded within the municipality, and the quota may be used as construction land in other localities of the municipality. Third, the claiming right of the land is held for the transferred households for three years in case they return for reasons of employment shock, etc. The unified utilization of the quota of land vacated by official migration from rural to urban areas is the motivation of Chongqing municipal government implementing the *hukou* reform.

The new round of *hukou* reform, represented by the experiences in Chongqing and Guangdong in 2010, meets the two criteria for reform — low threshold of entry and equal provision of social welfare. In Chongqing, those migrant workers who have worked and done business for a certain period of time, who buy houses, invest, or pay taxes of a certain amount within the destination cities, are eligible to obtain local *hukou* and to acquire equal access to employment assistance, social insurance, subsidized housing, education, medical care, etc. In Guangdong, the government converts various criteria into points, such as schooling, working skills, contributions to social insurance,

---

[5] The land voucher program, an innovative institution in Chongqing, is intended to unify land usage and development on a citywide basis. Namely, the administration issues vouchers for the increase of land area generated by reclaiming the house plots and collective construction land vacated by out-migration from villages and trading them in the government-run land exchange. Those who buy the vouchers get the quota of land use for non-agricultural development within the municipality.

volunteering, and blood donation, which are accumulated to obtain urban *hukou*. In these ways, becoming an urban citizen is no longer a random probability, but the outcome of a specific procedure.

Conclusions, Reflections, and Policy Suggestions

In the course of China's transition from planned economy to market economy, the *hukou* system reform has driven labor mobility from rural to urban sectors and helped the economy reallocate resources and gain efficiency as well as contributed to the unprecedented growth of the economy. However, under the constraints of unlimited supply of labor and scarcity of resources for public services, discrepancies in employment opportunities and welfare provisions among urban, migrant, and local workers have prevented the realization of reform, the completion of urbanization, and the floating urbanites from becoming a stable source of labor and consumption. As the Lewisian turning point arrives — that is, economic growth can no longer count on cheap labor and high savings rates brought by a demographic dividend — the central and local governments, seeking a new engine for economic growth, will set sights on the potential of deepening urbanization by settling migrant workers in urban areas. This creates incentives for governments implementing *hukou* reform, which are compatible between central and local governments and between migrant workers and urban native residents. As a result, *hukou* reform pushes forward in both breadth and width.

In the final analysis, different regions' governments have their own motives for carrying out *hukou* reform. They carry out reform to attract and keep human resources in coastal areas, to tap domestic demand in central and western regions, and to break through the land bottleneck in catching-up regions. The different motives have led to dissimilar institutional designs and ways of implementing. The diversity is not only the natural approach to such decentralized reform; it is also what the reform's advantage is based upon. Allowing diversity assures incentives, impetus, and chances of success.

Like the previous rounds of reform, the current ongoing reform has its limitations, which involve the consensus between central and local governments. That is, to initiate *hukou* reform, the local governments not only need incentives, but also legitimacy, in order to have the central government's support and approval. As can be seen in the experiences of Chongqing and Guangdong provinces, some shortcomings need to be overcome in this regard.

First, the point of intersection between the central government's top concern and the local governments' legitimacy in accelerating urbanization is to retain the designated amount of arable land. Due to the extreme scarcity of arable land in China, neither industrialization nor urbanization can proceed at the expense of shifting land from agricultural to non-agricultural use. The land voucher program, coined by the Chongqing government, must assure that all plots of land vacated are reclaimed for cultivation in order to be approbated by the central government. The central leaders often doubt the actual reclamation of land declared by local governments, because there have been too many cases of reneging in the process of new village construction.

Second, both the central government and the governments of the migrant-receiving cities are concerned about building labor market institutions and social protection mechanisms that prevent urban diseases. As the result of the advent of the Lewisian turning point, migrant workers have become an indispensable source of labor for urban sectors. In other words, non-agricultural sectors' demand for migrant workers has become unvarying, or rigid, and agriculture has been rapidly mechanized so that it no longer provides a pool of surplus labor. While migrant workers as a whole cannot revert to agricultural production, individual migrant workers risk becoming a part of the urban poor. So *hukou* reform must be a comprehensive package that tackles the risks, from inclusive social protection policy in urban areas to flexible relocation policy, of arable land.

Third, the coordination among policy measures undertaken by local governments and a holistic vision of the entire country impacts the overall effect of the reform. In the reforms of Chongqing and Guangdong provinces, policies set for migrant workers to officially reside in cities only benefit the residents of the specific province or municipality. In 2009, of the 145 million migrant workers (and their 22 million accompanying family members), 51% migrated across provincial boundaries. The fact that the inter-provincial migrants can hardly benefit from the currently *hukou* reform underway in many provinces implies that half of migrants, whose ancestral homes are mostly in the central and western poor areas, are still excluded from the urbanization process.

So far, the *hukou* reform has been the initiative of local governments motivated to break through the constraints of local development. As a public policy reform, *hukou* reform requires nationwide harmonization. That is, in addition to encouraging various local reform initiatives, the central government, by generalizing the domestic and international experiences and lessons, should also put forward a general guideline regarding the contents and coverage of social security programs, ways of managing vacated plots of land, and the nexus between the practical policies and overall objectives of the reform.

Chapter 6

Avoiding the Middle-Income Trap

6.1. Maintaining Sustainable Economic Growth Requires Giving Priority to the Development of Education

Giving priority to the development of education is important for economic growth and social development. The objective of educational reforms and development plans should proceed based on the actual conditions in the country and laws of education to realize the leap development of education. In addition, it should utilize the "education first" policy for promoting economic growth to the limit through defining education as the public good, extending education to enlarge the scale, reallocating resources to adjust the structure, opening up for competition to improve the quality, and following demand orientation to increase the efficiency.

Education as the source of economic growth

After the reform and opening-up, China gained competitiveness in labor-intensive products in the global market and the position of the world manufacturing center because of its advantage in labor quantity and education level. With higher labor costs in the eastern coastal areas, industry upgrade and industry transfer have begun. There are two essential aspects to China maintaining its competitiveness: (1) competitiveness is inversely related to labor cost; (2) competitiveness is proportionally related to labor productivity. With the emergence of the labor shortage and peoples' expectation of higher incomes, the rise of the wage rate is necessary and inevitable. Therefore, higher productivity, which is the result of higher education level, is essential for China to have a successful industrial structure adjustment and to avoid a crack of comparative advantages.

Our research shows that the labor productivity increases 17% as workers' education length increases one year in the manufacturing industry. Compared to the case that average workers in enterprises have a middle school diploma, the labor productivity may increase 24% if all workers have a high school diploma, and it increases 66% more if all workers are college graduates. In addition, there is a huge return for individuals to extend education, which implies the strong motivation for families to invest in education. Research shows that increasing the current urban and rural labor education length to 12 years, i.e., finishing high school, the return of education for urban workers increases 17% and the return of education for rural workers increases 21.1%. If the education length further increases to 14 years, the return of education for urban workers increases 41.2% and the return of education for rural workers increases 43.3%.

It is predicted that China's working-age population will reach the maximum around 2013 and start decreasing afterward, and the conventional demographic dividends that contribute to the economic growth will disappear. In the meantime, the population is aging and the resulting social pension burden will significantly increase. China should consider raising the real retirement age in the future to ensure labor supply, which almost fully depends on the development of education. In other words, developing education is the necessary condition to prepare for handling the aging population and creating the second demographic dividend.

Most developed countries handle the population aging through raising the mandatory retirement age. However, the precondition is that elderly workers' education level has no significant difference from young workers and their working experiences keep them competitive in the labor market. For example, in the American working-age population, a 20-year-old worker's average education length is 12.6 years, while a 60-year-old worker's average education length is 13.7 years. In China's current working-age population, older workers have lower education levels. For example, a 20-year-old Chinese worker's average education length is nine years, while a 60-year-old Chinese worker's average education length is only six years, the differences in education lengths increase from 29% for

20-year-old workers to 56% for 60-year-old workers compared to the American workers in the same age groups. When the retirement age is raised in this situation, elderly workers will become less competitive in the labor market.

Significantly raising the proportion of public investment in education for the "education first" policy

The current fiscal investment in education is 3.3% of China's GDP, which is 59% of the proportion in France, 79% of the proportion in Germany, 66% of the proportion in Britain, and 69% of the proportion in the U.S. China set the objective of increasing public investment in education based on this gap. However, it is necessary to set higher goals according to the following reasons.

First, a higher proportion of school-age population requires more public investment in education. The comparison above is not enough to show the real gap in the public education investment between China and other countries because the education investment scale is related to the demographic age structure of a country. Since the proportion of the school-age population is high in China, it should allocate more resources for education. According to the principle, we simulated a scenario using the proportion of school-age population in the U.S. as the benchmark. That is, we normalized the ratio of public expenditure in education to GDP. Because the proportion of school-age population is still high in China, the simulation results show that the public investment in education is only 2.8% of China's GDP, which is only 46% of the proportion in France, 52% of the proportion in Germany, 52% of the proportion in Britain, and 59% of the proportion in the U.S., so the gap with developed countries further increases.

Second, insufficient public investment in education restricts residents' regular consumptions. In developed countries, public fiscal expenditure accounts for 86% of society's total spending in education; the proportion is around 75% in developing countries, 80% on average in the world, but only 46% in China. In other words, using international standards, private investment is an extremely large proportion of the total education spending in China. Excessively depending on households to invest in education severely restricts private consumption and causes insufficient demands in other consumption aspects, which suppresses the inherent driving force for China's economic growth. It has important macroeconomic implications to expand public investment in education, especially when the financial crisis weakened exporting and investment demands. Insufficient public investment in education also results in the increasing inequality of education; the public complaints on education issues mainly stem from such a heavy burden of schooling on families.

Third, the critical minimum size of public education investment is the necessary condition for economic growth. Theoretically, the proportion of public education investment in GDP should follow an inverted U-shaped dynamic track. First, we observed that the proportion is low in developing countries, which is the result of low income per capita and insufficient resources and also the reason for their underdevelopment. In developing countries, the proportion of school-age population is high and the human capital stock level is low, realizing the leap development of education can accelerate the economic catch-up with developed countries, which requires a critical minimum size of public education investment. Second, because public education expenditures are mainly used for compulsory education, developed countries have gone beyond the stage of development to popularize compulsory education and the higher level requires more private investments. In the meantime, population is aging in developed countries and the proportion of school-age population is declining. Therefore, the proportion of public education investment tends to decrease, while the total education expenditure is still high in these countries. We did not observe the effect of this law in reality, because most developing countries have not realized excessive development of education and cannot significantly raise human capital to realize the economic catch-up.

More efficiently allocating education resources

Widespread research results show that the social benefit is the highest in preschool education, less high in school education, and the lowest in vocational education. It does not imply that the educational benefit decreases, but that when social benefit declines, private benefit rises in education.

Generally speaking, we define education as a public good. However, because the externality of education differs according to the supply type, China can follow the principles below to appropriately allocate public education resources and attract household expenditures on education.

First, fully keep the public good property of education, create conditions to include high school education in compulsory education, and give public support to preschool education. Because students' health in compulsory education has significant externality to the society, rural students' nutritional meals and urban students' athletic facilities are public goods, which the government should intervene.

Second, vocational education and adult education are quasi-public goods, because the state is in debt to those generations who experienced "cultural revolution" and "sent down to the countryside," and such types of education can yield private return to individuals and enterprises. Therefore, China should encourage society, enterprises, and households to invest, in addition to public support.

Because the main inputs of education resources are diversified, we can integrate education resources to more efficiently utilizing them in the current stage of development. In recent years, the aggregate inputs of education resources from household, social, and fiscal investments continually increase. In 2006, household investment accounted for 45.3% of the total education resources and the proportion was 5% for social investment and 49.7% for fiscal investment. Although public finance continually increases inputs for education, the household investment scale is still large. It also implies the potential to integrate the current education resources through extending education institutional reforms and bringing in the open and competitive educational system.

Realizing the leap development of education requires a significant increase in public investment and promotion in social justice through education equalization with inclined distribution of incremental resources. As basic public services, education, especially compulsory education, in China by and large lacks equity. Researches show that income differentials are still large in China's labor market because of the high return rate of education. It is the result of the labor market development and also reflects that equal education opportunities and equal education resource allocations are important means to realizing social justice and reducing income differentials. Therefore, China should mainly use incremental educational resources for the construction of equal education services, while at the same time increase public inputs of education resources.

6.2. How to Deal with the Challenge of "Growing Old Before Becoming Rich"

According to the United Nation's prediction, the increment of China's working-age population will gradually decrease and become zero between 2000 and 2015. Meanwhile, the proportion of elderly population above 65 years old will increase from 6.8% to 9.6%, and the elderly population will exceed 130 million by the end of the 12th five-year plan. The relationship between China's economic growth and demographic transition can be characterized as "growing old before becoming rich," which was observed as a general phenomenon, but has many implications, especially its effect on economic growth. Therefore, observing the most important challenge in the 12th five-year plan from this angle helps us to seek out the new source for keeping sustainable economic growth.

"Growing old before becoming rich" and the middle-income trap

Generally speaking, richer countries have a larger proportion of aging population. Therefore, China does not need to worry about getting old. However, China is experiencing the unusual problem of "growing old before becoming rich." In recent years, the catch-up of China's aggregate economic volume and GDP per capita both accelerated. For example, China's GDP per capita was one-fifth of the world average level in 2000. It is currently 47.7% of the world average and the aggregate economic volume is ranked second in the world. Meanwhile, the proportion of aging population is also catching up. In 2000, elderly people above 65 years accounted for 6.8% of the total population, which was equal to the world average level. However, in 2010, the proportion increased to 8.9% while the world average level was 7.5%. In other words, China's aging population has significantly caught up.

Is there any way to stop or reverse the trend of population aging? In my opinion, it is impossible. Changes in the demographic age structure are not caused by any single policy, but because of the demographic transition corresponding to stage of economic development. Developed countries in early stages, and many other developing countries, have gone through this process. Therefore, policy improvement and adjustment are undoubtedly necessary but not helpful to completely deter the trend of population aging in the long term. Accelerating economic growth is the most important among all China's tasks. If China compares itself with high-income countries instead of developing countries 10 or 20 years later, then China is not old, but relatively young, and the key is how China can close the gap of "growing old before becoming rich." China's GDP per capita exceeded USD 4,000 in 2010 and is predicted to exceed USD 6,000 by the end of the 12th five-year plan and approach USD 12,000, the income per capita level of high-income countries, in 2020 if the growth rate in the past 30 years is applied.

Another concept is the middle-income trap. So far, literature has discussed the phenomenon, which is the content of the middle-income trap, such as economic stagnation, income distribution aggravation, etc. However, from initial discussions about the mechanism of the middle-income trap in economic literatures, we can find many similarities between the middle-income trap and the problem of "growing old before becoming rich." It is said that China faces the danger of falling into the middle-income trap, because, economists found that the two economic extremes (very poor countries and very rich countries) benefit the most from the globalization. According to the ranking of countries, countries' benefits from the globalization can be represented by a U-shaped curve, the shape of which is more obvious if comparing with the inverted U-shaped curve before the globalization.

It is simple to explain the phenomenon with economic theories. Poor countries have the comparative advantage in abundant and inexpensive labor and can gain globalization dividends by producing and selling the most inexpensive labor-intensive products in the global market. Rich countries have higher management and technology innovation capabilities and have the comparative advantage in capital-intensive and technology-intensive industries, which can be fulfilled in globalization. According to conventional comparative advantage theories, every country has its own comparative advantage, but the comparative advantage is not significant if it is not a very poor or very rich country. Therefore, these countries benefit less from globalization, have worse performance in economic growth, and even fall into the middle-income trap.

The close of the demographic opportunity window

Let us observe the implication of "growing old before becoming rich." "Growing old," i.e., the rapid change in demographic age structure, implies that the endowments structure has changed, labor has become more expensive, and capital has become relatively cheaper, but still not abundant, which means that the previous comparative advantage in labor-intensive industries is lost. "Before becoming rich" implies that we cannot gain significant comparative advantages in capital-intensive and technology-intensive industries in the short term. Therefore, China is in an embarrassing situation based on its comparative advantages in the current stage of development. In another inaccurate way, we face the "comparative advantage vacuum." Although we do not have the real comparative advantage vacuum, but only insignificant comparative advantage, the previous economic growth pattern cannot support sustainable economic growth. However, whether China will fall into the middle-income trap depends on its policy choices.

Let us further analyze China's challenge of "growing old before becoming rich." So far, the characteristics of China's demographic age structure are the large amount and high proportion of working-age population, which guarantee sufficient labor supply, create conditions for high saving rate, and provide demographic dividends for the economic growth since the 1980s after the reform and opening-up was initiated. According to our estimates, the decrease of the demographic dependency ratio has contributed to 26.8% of the growth of GDP per capita between 1982 and 2000. However, the demographic dividends are disappearing.

We also call the stage of development with demographic dividends the "demographic opportunity window," which lasts until the end of the declining trend of demographic dependency ratio. Demographic dependency ratio is defined as using the dependent population below 16 years old and above 65 years old as the numerator and the working-age population between 16 years old and 64 years old as the denominator, calculating the ratio of these two groups. It is necessary to see what challenges China is facing in comparison with the arrival time of other East Asian countries. In the early 1960s, Japan met the same labor shortage and the wage-increasing trend that are currently occurring in China. That is, labor supply is no longer unlimited, and the disappearance of such a most significant characteristic of dual economy indicates the passage of the Lewis turning point. South Korea met the Lewis turning point around 1970.

Suppose that China meets the Lewis turning point today (though 2004 would have been the year meeting this point in my opinion), let us compare the close of the demographic opportunity window with other Asian countries. Japan's demographic dividends disappeared after 1990, and its demographic dependency ratio reached the minimum in 1995 and started to increase afterward. In 2015, South Korea will close the demographic opportunity window at almost the same time as China, i.e., its demographic dependency ratio will reach the minimum and rapidly lose demographic dividends. Demographic dividends in Thailand will also disappear at almost the same time as China. However, the current income per capita in China is only 25% of that in South Korea and is slightly lower than that in Thailand. Let us compare with the countries that have lower income levels than China, such as India and Vietnam, which still have years left to benefit from demographic dividends. In conclusion, all countries that are more developed and less developed can have significant comparative advantages in either capital and technology or labor, but China's demographic opportunity window closes too early and the window of the new comparative advantage is not yet open.

Characterizing China's development stage

There are some phenomena caused by "growing old" or the premature demographic transition. First of all, labor supply or the new increment of working-age population will rapidly drop to zero during the 12th five-year plan. We use the working-age population between 16 years and 64 years old as the broad term of labor supply. Accurately speaking, people younger than 16 years are not in the labor market and people older than

60 years are also out of the labor market, according to the mandatory retirement age rule in China. However, even using the broad term of labor supply, the migrant rural labor supply cannot fulfill the demand in the urban labor market in China during the 12th five-year plan. The two groups (i.e., the migrant rural labor as supply side and the urban employment as demand side) will offset each other and the increment of China's working-age population will become zero and start to decrease after 2013. The changing relationship of labor supply and labor demand and the continual occurrence of labor shortage are reflections of "growing old."

Correspondingly, we observe that average workers' wage increasingly rises. No matter whether, non-agricultural industries that mainly reflect full-time workers' wages, such as the construction industry and the manufacturing industry, or for peasant workers and paid workers in agriculture, in general, wages started to rapidly increase after 2004. For example, the annual growth rate of peasant workers' wages is, on average, more than 10% and the amount of wage increases for workers in agriculture is even larger. When there is the same trend in several sectors, the conclusion is clear: it is not a temporary phenomenon or because of structural reasons, but the wage increase is because of the labor shortage and should be a trend in the long term.

In the meantime, we observe that though there have always been shortages in technical workers and skilled workers at any time, the current phenomenon is the shortages in unskilled workers, which results in the rapid wage increase of average workers and significant wage convergence between skilled labor and unskilled labor. The wage convergence results in negative incentives for education. With more careful econometric analysis, we will find that the return of education to education among peasant workers is declining. For example, using middle-school education as the benchmark, the relative return of high school education and higher education significantly increased in the period of 2005 to 2010. In other words, the wage convergence is good for reducing income differentials but not for motivating the youth to stay at schools. For average families, especially poor families, there is not only direct cost for education, but also opportunity cost for delayed employment, and higher opportunity cost may cause people not attending school or dropping out over a period of time.

There are also several important examples of "before becoming rich," or that China is at a relatively low economic growth period. First of all, the World Bank predicted China's potential growth rate. Because China's employment grows more slowly, its contribution to economic growth significantly drops and will be trivial during the 12th five-year plan and become negative during the 13th five-year plan, lowering the potential growth rate. So far, the real growth rate has not declined because of the government-led investment and the stimulus package. In addition, the regional development strategy is capital-intensive, implying that China supports the current growth rate with the increase of capital labor ratio, which is not sustainable in the future. The contribution of human capital does not significantly change and the growth rate of total factor productivity will not significantly increase in the future. The assumption used by World Bank experts is optimistic; many other researchers conclude that China's total factor productivity did not perform well, or was even negative, after the mid-1990s. Therefore, without the significant support of the total factor productivity, the potential growth rate will inevitably decline in the future.

There are other aspects that reflect "before becoming rich." One is that the demand for labor quality may not be fulfilled during the industry structural upgrade. Despite the negative incentive for education, human capital endowments significantly decrease as the age of the current labor stock increases, which is in vivid contrast to the situation in Japan and the U.S., where the education levels of all age groups remain constant. In addition, though China is ranked 27th for its competitiveness in the Global Competitiveness Report (2010–2011), it is mainly because of China's macroeconomic stability and the market size. Meanwhile, China is ranked lower for its technology level. For example, it is ranked 57th for its financial market maturity, 60th for its higher education and trainings, and 78th for its technology readiness. This reveals that China still has a huge gap in education and technology compared to developed countries.

Policy suggestions

A middle-income country is not guaranteed to smoothly become one of the high-income countries. Instead, it may face the danger of falling into the middle-income trap. China faces similar challenges when dealing with the problem of "growing old before becoming rich." On one hand, as the relative scarcity of production factors has changed, the conventional comparative advantage has gradually disappeared; on the other hand, income per capita is still low and the new comparative advantage has not been revealed. Therefore, maintaining factors and exploiting new sources that support the growth of total factor productivity requires China to change the economic development pattern. For China's current policy choice, it is most important to extend the existing comparative advantage to its maximum, avoid the shock therapy-type adjustment, and keep on the right track of economic development pattern transition and industry structural upgrade. We raise several urgent policy suggestions to achieve the goal.

First of all, China should accelerate the transition of economic growth to the domestic demand-driven pattern. Why is it urgent? On one hand, demand inevitably decreases because the comparative advantage changes in the middle-income stage. Although industrial structure adjustment can take the gradual approach with changes of the resource endowments structure, developed countries recover slowly after the global financial crisis and the rebalance adjustment of the global economy tends to reduce the demand of major importing countries, "jobless recovery," and the rising protectionism in the U.S. also suppress the growth of China's exports. Therefore, adjusting China's economy is an urgent task. Following the objective requirement of the development stage and the particular trend of the global economy, China's economic growth should turn to the domestic demand-driven pattern, especially the final consumption demand-driven pattern, to realize economic rebalance and sustainable economic growth.

On the other hand, domestic demand is adaptive to China's current production structure, industry structure, and resource endowments structure. Therefore, China does not have to accept the shock therapy-type industrial structure adjustment and can avoid the comparative advantage vacuum. In expanding domestic demand, China can continue to utilize the existing production capacity and gain additional time for industrial structure adjustment. According to the classification by the Asian Development Bank and using the purchasing power parity (PPP), the middle-income population, whose daily average consumption is between two and 20 dollars, account for 66% of the total population and their consumption accounts for 79.2% of the total consumption in China.

The characteristics show that: (1) The middle-income residents, which make a large portion of the total population, are still a group with relatively low incomes and their consumption level is adaptive to current industrial structure and exporting structure or the low-end commodities in China; (2) Because their consumption is a large proportion of the total consumption, with the expansion of the group, their consumption demand can support the domestic demand-driven economic growth for a long time.

Second, China should realize the industrial transfer from the coastal regions to central and western regions and build up the domestic "flying geese" model. Although the comparative advantage in labor-intensive industries is gradually lost in the east regions, shifting labor-intensive industries to the central and western regions can extend the comparative advantage for a period of time. China has a large territory, so when the labor cost rises in one region, it may remain low in other regions for quite a long time. Data from the National Statistics Bureau shows that although wage levels in the east, middle, and west regions are converging, workers are not willing to work without wage increase, or they frequently negotiate for wage increases in the coastal areas, while the wage level is still favorable in the central and western regions since migrant workers are willing to work near their home. Therefore, labor-intensive industries still have space to develop in the inland areas. In addition, the increase of total factor productivity has been gained through the increase of resource reallocation efficiency rather than the increase of the micro-perspective technological efficiency in the past. If China can build up the "flying-geese" model, it will continue to gain resource reallocation efficiency.

Therefore, it is important to improve the investment environment in the central and western regions. Instead of solely increasing investment or subsidy, the government should promote the institutional reforms in these regions to retain their comparative advantage and the sustainable economic catch-up in the long term and to avoid the fate of "lost two decades" in Japan and the "Mezzogiorno trap" in Europe. In the implementation of the current regional development strategy, the rapid increase of capital intensity of manufacturing in the central and western regions should call

China's attention. During 2000 and 2007, the annual growth rate of capital–labor ratio in manufacturing industries was 4.2% in the east region, 9.2% in the central region, and 8.1% in the west region. In 2007, capital–labor ratios in the central region and the west region were 20.1% and 25.9% higher than that in the east region, respectively.

Third, China should fully recognize the resource endowment characteristics in the middle-income stage in order to avoid the all-around technological catch-up. Technology develops with "two legs." On one hand, China should realize the leap catch-up in the frontier technology areas that have narrower gaps with developed countries. In particular, China should utilize its high-speed economic growth and the market potential of the huge aggregate economic volume to make breakthroughs in the strategic emerging technologies. On the other hand, China should objectively and accurately recognize its resource endowment characteristics based on the current stage of economic development, fully utilize the technological gap between China and developed countries, and retain the advantage of backwardness through innovating applicable technologies and absorbing and bringing in foreign technologies. Currently, medium and small-size enterprises, which account for 98% of the enterprises in China, own or collect too few research and development funds and the proportion of the funds is decreasing over the years, which is not in favor of applicable technology innovations.

6.3. The Crux of the Continually Increasing Income Inequality

Society paid great attention to the huge income differentials between regions, industries, and groups of residents, and the central government made the deployment to "further adjust the national income distribution and enhance the consumption capability of residents and especially the low-income group." China has entered the transition period from a middle-income country to a high-income country, so how to solve the income distribution disparity problem and avoid the middle-income trap is relevant to the great goal of realizing a generally affluent society by 2020. Although all of society has paid attention to the enlarged income differentials, there is no agreement on the reason for the current income distribution situation and problems. In this section, the author is going to clarify several questions through summarizing China's reform and development process and other countries' experiences and lessons.

Reducing income inequality through responsible public policy

The Gini coefficient of the residents' income has exceeded the fire line of 0.4 in 2002, and the trend has not been held back or called enough attention so far. The correct diagnosis should be made before solving this chronic problem: what factors lead to the enlarged income differentials; how to narrow the income differentials; which means can be applied to positively achieve this goal; which method should be used with cautions; what should be avoided; and how to draw up the correct income distribution policy and effectively reduce income differentials.

Many people think that income differentials are the result of market competition or the reflection of human capital differentials in the market economy and its existence should not be surprising. This point of view ignores the fact that public policies should play a role in the income distribution. The income distribution should be equal and efficient in the market economy, especially because many income differentials come from unequal opportunities. Therefore, we cannot simply consider it as an economic phenomenon. Even in capitalist countries, governments cannot fully ignore the income distribution problem. For example, the American economist Paul Krugman reviewed the relationship of different policy tendencies toward income distribution and the real income disparity levels during the alternative administrations of the Democratic Party and the Republican Party in the U.S. and concluded that the income distribution policy is relevant to, and has significant effect on, the income distribution.

Another point of view is that many people consider the improvement of income distribution as the wage increase, implying that the government should intervene in wage decisions. However, in diversified economic sectors, it is the enterprise's major authority to decide wages. In the micro perspective, depriving the authority of wage decision means the deprivation of the enterprise's autonomy in operation and management. In the more macro perspective, increasing the efficiency of human capital allocation should utilize the function of the labor market and intervening in wage decisions implies harm to the market institution and conflicts with average workers' fundamental interests.

Therefore, solving the problem of increasing income differentials is primarily the responsibility of the government. The government should apply a series of public policies for comprehensive treatment. This includes improving equal education and avoiding intergenerational transmission of poverty; implementing proactive employment policy, guaranteeing equal, decent, and sufficient employment; developing labor market institutions, protecting workers' rights, and constructing harmonic labor relations; building up well-covered social security system and providing residents safeguard for basic living. In the meantime, the government should be accurately aware of its authority, maintain appropriate functions, avoid going beyond its duty or even sacrificing the fundamental role of market resource allocation.

Equal employment is the necessary condition for reducing income differentials

China should follow the transition from a middle-income country to a high-income country, maintain sustainable economic growth, and continue to expand urban and rural residents' employment. Realizing equal and sufficient employment is the precondition for China to increase income and improve income distribution. Since the 1990s, a large number of surplus rural labor migrated for work and the number of peasant workers who have worked outside of their area for more than six months reached 145 million in 2009. Income differentials between urban and rural workers are overestimated, because the income of migrant peasant workers is ignored in the statistics; income differentials would have been significantly reduced if peasant workers' income was taken into the calculation. The author does not intend to deny the existence of income differentials between urban and rural households, but wants to show that increasing employment participation in non-agricultural wage sectors is the fundamental method and necessary condition to increase the income of average workers and low-income families and further improve the overall income distribution.

Improving income distribution requires China to increase the proportion of workers' income in the primary national income distribution and it eventually depends on the continual expansion of employment. When labor supply exceeds labor demand, sufficient employment becomes more difficult. Therefore, the average worker's income grows slowly for a long period of time. Only when employment opportunity significantly increases and the relationship of labor supply and labor demand is significantly improved can conditions for increasing the overall wage level mature. In recent years, with sufficient rural labor migration, labor shortages emerged and China reached the Lewis turning point. According to the law of supply and demand in the labor market, it is reasonable to observe that average workers' income gradually increases and income differentials start to decrease.

Employment is not the sufficient condition for reducing income differentials. Although the labor market reacts to the relationship of labor supply and labor demand with its own adjustment mechanism, the government can also play a role in increasing workers' wages and increasing the proportion of worker's remuneration in the primary distribution beyond market forces. First of all, the government should maintain fair competition in the labor market and clear the entry barriers in different industries. This includes eliminating sector monopoly and enterprise monopoly, preventing discrimination in the labor market, avoiding the effect of non-competitive factors on residents' income and the income differentials caused by non-human capital factors. Second, through the household registration system reform, the government should eliminate the link between public services and the household registration system and further reduce barriers for labor migration between urban and rural areas, between sectors, and between enterprises. Lastly, the government should prevent the violation of labor legislations and incidences that harm workers' rights.

Rights protection is the institutional guarantee for reducing income differentials

Lack of rights protection and the informality of the labor market produce the income differentials. Unlike in the products market, humans are the carriers of the labor force, therefore, the management and regulation of the labor market should be different from that in the product market. For example, the minimum wage system can be a powerful leverage if it is applied appropriately. In recent years, local governments gradually raised the minimum wage standard, making it an important means to regulate average workers' wage. Since the 1990s, more cities have adjusted the minimum wage standard and the annual growth of the minimum wage standard has accelerated.

In order to deal with the financial crisis and promote employment and reemployment, China temporarily suspended the minimum wage adjustment in 2009. With the employment situation improving, especially after the emergence of the new "peasant worker shortage," China's provinces and cities restarted the adjustment in 2010.

We should point out that the initial objective of the minimum wage regime is to protect workers' rights, rather than for the government to intervene in wage decisions in the market economy. Therefore, the decision-making and the adjustment frequency of the standard should refer to the market equilibrium level. It may harm the hiring enthusiasm of the enterprises and create negative effects on the expansion of employment if exceeding the level.

Through the construction of labor market institutions, especially the tri-party consultation mechanism and the collective wage bargaining system, China can achieve the goal of increasing wages and protecting workers. It is an inaccurate recognition that wage should be fully determined by labor supply and labor demand. In fact, whether wage decisions depend more on the spontaneous labor market or labor market institutions reflects the stages of economic development and the labor market development level. The general law is that the labor market spontaneously determines the wage rate when labor supply exceeds labor demand, while labor market institutions play a more important role in wage decisions with a more balanced relationship of labor supply and labor demand and even the emergence of labor shortages. We can affect the labor market through the institutions construction because workers, enterprises, and the government can implement the tri-party consultation, which is in favor of resolving the contradictions in labor relations and can prevent excessive intervention to the labor market. It is worth utilizing the institutional arrangement and its implementation should be accelerated.

Potentials to reduce income differentials in the redistribution area

Because of the existence of unfair institutions and unequal opportunities, as well as vulnerable groups in economic activities, it is necessary to correct and adjust the primary distribution result through reasonable redistributions. China can start improving the social redistribution mechanism through reforming the tax system, eliminating entry barriers, and expanding equal public services.

First of all, China should promote social equalization through tax system reforms. In the new stage of development with labor shortages, local governments' enthusiasm of promoting local economic growth has transitioned policy orientation and government function from attracting investment to attracting human resources. The later orientation requires the government to provide more, better, and more equal public services. The tax system reform should follow this trend, shaping a correspondence between fiscal capability and administrative responsibility of local governments — that is, having more revenue inclined to localities and communities.

Second, unequal entry opportunities will result in monopoly profits and further cause huge income differentials among workers engaged in different industries. China should bring a larger proportion of the state-owned enterprise profits into government revenue, instead of the internal distribution or reinvestment by the profitable enterprises. For example, for natural monopolistic industries, China should use monopoly profits as national income, or as regulatory tax to subsidize the low-income group or in other forms to increase residents' property income.

Third, China should improve the personal income tax to be more progressive. The tax should not target the low-income and middle-income groups, because it will suppress the formation and expansion of the middle-income group. Although personal income tax does not account for a large proportion of the total tax amount, it has a significant effect on low-income families. Meanwhile, the high-income group has a variety of means to avoid tax. Therefore, China should determine its reform, by not only significantly increasing the threshold level of the tax, but also transforming the personal income tax basis from the personal income tax to more progressive taxes, such as property tax.

Finally, the government should provide all residents with equal public services in aspects such as different social insurances, social assistance, compulsory education, and the construction and supply of other social infrastructures. The sufficient supply and wide coverage of these services can not only raise residents' income but also eliminate workers and low-income families' worries on accident shocks and increase their consumption proportions and consumption levels. The current social security system has the regressive nature that the overall coverage is relatively low and more vulnerable groups in the labor market have less social security coverage. Therefore, China should be dedicated to expand the coverage of public services, build up the subsistence allowance system, social assistance and basic pension insurance on the tax security basis and allow them to cover all residents.

6.4. Extended Reading: Is There a "Middle-Income Trap?" China's Theories, Experiences, and Importance

Abstract: Through the review of relevant studies and analysis, this section indicates that the "middle-income trap" is in line with the framework of the mainstream economic growth theories, and therefore, it is a useful concept through which we can analyze economic growth phenomena in specific economic growth phases. The empirical experiences of many countries also indicate that, at specific middle-income stages, economies with high growth rates tend to encounter economic slowdown or even stagnation. This section shows that China is facing the challenge of determining how to move smoothly beyond the middle-income stage of economic development, while taking into account the shifting population structure, changing resource endowment, and growth patterns. Drawing on international experiences, it also puts forward several policy suggestions relating to improvement in total factor productivity, expansion of human capital accumulation and deepening of the system, and government function reforms.

Introduction

Based on the view that East Asia is the most dynamic region in the world, the World Bank conducts a theme study of the East Asian economy every four years to summarize its unique development experiences and lessons and to expose problems and challenges over specific time spans. In its 2007 report, *An East Asian Renaissance: Ideas for Economic Growth*, the World Bank, for the first time, raised the issue of a "middle-income trap" (Indermit Gill *et al.*, 2008). The report showed that "middle-income countries have grown less rapidly than either rich or poor countries" (p. 5).

Since then, the concept of the middle-income trap has increasingly been discussed among economists. It has been used to illustrate the predicaments of certain Latin American and Asian economies, and is applied as a reference for making judgments on China's economic prospects (Wang *et al.*, 2009; Eichengreen *et al.*, 2011; Kharas, 2011). Its relevance to China's case, meanwhile, has drawn more attention since the Chinese Ministry of Finance, the Development Research Center of the State Council, and the World Bank jointly conducted a study on how China can overcome the middle-income trap.

Meanwhile, many researchers disagree on the use of the concept of the middle-income trap. Although systematic research is not yet available, in what follows, we touch on the nature of such disagreements. First, some researchers hold that the word "trap" is improper, because it suggests "conspiracy." How can an economy be framed? Second, some economists think that, unlike the theory of poverty trap or vicious circle of poverty, there is no economic theory available that can explain the many phenomena related to the so-called middle-income trap. Third, some suppose that the middle-income trap theory lacks empirical evidence. It is also pointed out that over the past 40 years, growth performance of middle-income countries has not been significantly lower than that of high-income and low-income countries. Finally, some researchers doubt the issue's relevance to China: Does the concept of the middle-income trap correctly depict China's challenges and will it help China find the right solutions?

A concept or proposition is worth bringing forward so long as it can be analyzed through theoretical frameworks, and has significant empirical evidence and specific relevance, so that more thorough discussion and studies can be carried out. For that reason, this section supports the concept of the middle-income trap and holds that relevant studies should be deepened. Part 2 of this section starts, with a review of economic theories, of economic growth theories in particular, and demonstrates that the middle-income trap can certainly be included in existing economic growth analysis frameworks or has the potential of forming a special framework of its own. The third subsection introduces some empirical studies and statistical proofs of the middle-income trap and summarizes relevant characteristics of the concept. Finally, by introducing characteristics of China's economic development phase, the fourth subsection discusses the implications of the concept of middle-income trap to China's sustainable economic growth.

Theoretical Basis of Middle-Income Trap

Traditionally, the word "trap" is used to describe an economic state of superstable equilibrium that is beyond a comparative static equilibrium and cannot be changed by normal short-term outside forces. In other words, after the effect of a factor that helps improve per capita income is fully emerged, because it is somewhat unsustainable, other restraining factors will begin to work and offset that effect, bringing per capita income back to the original level. For example, the pessimistic views of Thomas Robert Malthus on the relationship between population growth and economic development are reflected in the "Malthusian trap" or the "Malthusian equilibrium." R. R. Nelson went further to combine the Malthusian model with the Harrod–Domar growth model to form a development theory, which uses the low-level equilibrium trap as a label of the less-developed countries (Hayami *et al.*, 2009). Moreover, not only is absolute poverty an equilibrium state; some economic historians have put forward the hypothesis of "high-level equilibrium trap" when attempting to explain China's historical development and fix the Needham Puzzle. Therefore, the use of the term "equilibrium trap" has a long history in development economics.

This concept is conducive for deducing policy implications from theoretical analyses. Based on the low-level equilibrium trap hypothesis, development economics has developed the "critical minimum effort" and the "big-push" theories, among other explanatory theories, as well as their corresponding policy implications. Another example is from Theodore W. Schultz (1999), who sees the traditional agriculture that is normal in developing countries also as a state of equilibrium, based on which he derives policy suggestions on reforming traditional agriculture through introducing new factors of production to break the equilibrium.

However, the aforementioned development economic theories concerning equilibrium state that this analysis has not been incorporated into mainstream growth theories. In reality, mainstream economists have long since separated the neoclassical analysis of economic growth from the development facts observed based on the above hypotheses. Despite this, Hansen and Prescott (2002) attempt to meld the Malthusian equilibrium model and Solow's neoclassical growth model and analyze them using a unified theoretical framework. They also notice that there is a transitional phase from the Malthusian model to the Solow model. Logically, we can certainly define that transitional phase as a unique economic development phase. In reality, the dual economy defined by Arthur Lewis is just a transitional state between the Malthusian poverty trap and the Solow neoclassical growth model and is prevalent in developing countries. In this phase, economic growth has gone beyond the vicious poverty cycle in which income growth leads to population increase, which, in turn, drags the income level down to a basic subsistence level, and entered a phase characterized by modern sectors continually absorbing agricultural surplus labor until the economy encounters the Lewis turning point, so that there is no longer an unlimited supply of labor, and becomes more and more neoclassical-like.

Aoki (2011) divides the economic development in East Asia into the Malthusian phase of the poverty trap (M-phase), the government-led development phase (G-phase), the Kuznets process in which development is realized through structural shifts (K-phase), the human capital-based development phase (H-phase), and the post-demographic transition phase (PD-phase). He also acknowledges that the Kuznets phase can be called the Lewis development phase, or the Kuznets–Lewis phase. The division of development phases reveals that the shift from one development phase to another means a jump or breach, or, in other words, while shaking off the poverty trap is an important step, the shifts from middle-income to high-income levels (from the K-phase to H-phase and ultimately the PD-phase) are equally important jumps. If the latter is so challenging that some economies have long failed to break through this phase, and the phenomenon is so widespread that it has had statistical significance and entails important theoretical and policy implications, then it is logical for us to use the concept of the middle-income trap.

Researchers have noticed some stylized facts that can help economists form an initial theoretical framework to conceptualize the middle-income trap. Eeckhout and Jovanovic (2007) compare the economic growth of various economies before and after globalization, and find that in the era of globalization, the long-term growth rate track of those economies, if they are ranked using the criterion of per capita income, would be U-shaped. An explanation in this study is that laborers in rich countries possess better technologies and skills, so the number of high-skill positions have grown, particularly with the global shift in economic structures, whereas poor countries do not have the same level of skills, but the number of unskilled jobs has increased; those countries in between, meanwhile, do not have either of these labor resource advantages. Garrett (2004) goes further to explain that when rich countries become increasingly affluent because of their accelerating technological advancement, the poorest countries have achieved faster growth in their manufacturing, but those countries in between fail to make headway.

This, in reality, hints at a general theoretical explanation for the middle-income trap; that is, countries at higher economic development stages obviously gain from globalization due to their comparative advantages in capital-intensive and technology-intensive industries thanks to their technological innovation capabilities. As a result of their rich labor resources and low labor costs, those at lower economic development stages also gain from globalization given their comparative advantages in labor-intensive industries. Those middle-income countries in between, however, gain less from globalization because they do not have comparative advantages in either aspect. We summarize this scenario as a "comparative advantage vacuum," which, although not completely accurate, helps to illustrate the uncomfortable situation the middle-income countries are facing.

In addition, according to the economic growth convergence hypothesis (Barro and Sala-i-Martin, 1995), economic growth depends on multiple factors, such as investment ratio, human capital accumulation, government function, infrastructure conditions, and system and policy environments. In other words, at the initial development phase of low per capita income, improvements in these factors propel economic growth convergence. However, the accumulation or improvement of those growth-favorable elements is also subject to the law of diminishing marginal effects; when all the "low-hanging fruits" have been harvested, the exogenous forces pushing economic growth will gradually lose their luster, unless the economy successfully shifts to an endogenous growth model driven mainly by total factor productivity. However, such a hypothesis generally applies to an economy that has entered the phase of a high-income country. Therefore, as the 2007 World Bank report indicated, development strategies and policies that are starkly different from previous ones must be adopted during a country's transition from the middle-income to the high-income phase (Indermit Gill *et al.*, 2008).

Empirical Evidence of the Middle-Income Trap

According to the categorization of the World Bank in recent years, calculated by the "atlas method" that is similar to the method for market exchange rate, those with per capita gross national income (GNI) of lower than USD 975 are in the low income group, whereas those with per capita GNI of USD 976 to USD 3855 are categorized as belonging to the lower-middle income group; those with per capita GNI of USD 3856 to USD 11,905 belong to the upper-middle income group and those with per capita GNI of more than USD 11,906 are high income countries. Of course, the standards of categorization are dynamic. Based on similar dynamic standards, if a country steps into the rank of middle-income countries but fails to advance and become a high-income country after a long period of growth, then it falls into the middle-income trap.

According to such standards, in reality, if countries that have become rich through oil exports are excluded, apart from the developed economies, such as the U.S. and European countries, so far only Japan, Korea, Singapore, Chinese Taiwan, Hong Kong, and Macao have successfully surpassed the middle-income group. Many Latin American countries, which once had similar development levels to European countries, as well as some Asian countries that have long been middle-income countries, have failed to become members of the high-income group. Even some Latin American countries whose per capita incomes once crossed the demarcation line between middle-income and high-income groups have ultimately retrogressed to the middle-income levels.

Due to technological advancement, institutional innovation, and strengthened resource mobilization capabilities, the world's production frontier has been expanding over time. Therefore, it is more appropriate to use relative, instead of absolute, per capita income to categorize income groups and, in particular, to examine the middle-income trap as a phenomenon of lingering growth. Athukorala and Woo (2011) used the purchasing power parity method of economic historian Angus Maddison to estimate the per capita GDP of particular economies and to compile the Catch-Up Index (CUI), with values presented as a percentage of the U.S. level of per capita GDP. Using this method, the authors prove, to an extent, the existence of the middle-income trap.

To be exact, they define those with a CUI higher than 55% as high-income countries, those with a CUI between 20% and 55% as middle-income countries, and those with a CUI lower than 20% as low-income countries. Among the 132 countries being compared, there were 32 middle-income countries in 1960, compared to 24 in 2008. Changes in the group show that there is a 50% possibility of the middle-income countries remaining in the middle-income trap. Considering cross-group movement, the possibility of moving to the lower level is higher than that of moving upward. Although there are countries from other groups moving into the middle-income group, the number of countries moving upward from the low-income group doubles that of those moving downward from the high-income group.

Some studies reveal the formation of the middle-income trap from a dynamic perspective. For example, they summarize statistics of concerned economies and find that in the middle-income phase, a country's economic growth would not perpetually maintain its growth momentum. Therefore, the study of phases in which economic growth generally slows down can verify the existence of the middle-income trap. Morgan Stanley Asia/Pacific economists have conducted such a study (Wang *et al.*, 2009). Through studying world economic history, they find that the growth of an economy will slow down after some years of high growth. The turning point of the process comes when purchasing power parity-based per capita GDP reaches USD 7000. From the study of economic historian Angus

Maddison, they find that over the past 100 years, 40 economies have seen their per capita GDP reach the turning point of USD 7000, 31 of which saw their growth rates decline by 2.8 percentage points on average after reaching that turning point.

Another study, conducted by Eichengreen *et al.* (2011), digs deeper into an analysis of relevant statistics. The question to be answered by this study is when or at what per capita income level a fast-growing economy would see its growth slow. They find from international comparisons that based on the purchasing power parity method and the dollar value in 2005, when the per capita income reaches USD 17,000, the fast-growing economy would normally encounter an obvious slowdown, with its average annual economic growth rate generally declining by 2 percentage points.

There are also studies that attempt to prove that the middle-income trap is non-existent. Investment bank economist Jonathan Anderson (2011) chooses 10 "middle-income countries" with a per capita income of USD 8000–10,000 and 10 "low-income countries" with a per capita income of USD 1000–3000, and compares their long-term economic performance. His findings can be summarized as follows: First, "middle-income countries" performed well in the first decade of this century, despite the fact that they stagnated during the previous decade. Second, "low-income countries" have failed to show better growth performance compared with their middle-income counterparts. Third, the average growth rates of the countries in both groups are almost the same. From these findings, Anderson comes to the conclusion that the middle-income trap does not exist. In reality, however, his data and interpretation are not adequate for him to come to such a conclusion. First, his categorization of the two groups of countries differs from the typical income-based categorization. For example, his grouping of "middle-income countries" includes both the former planned-economy countries and those Latin American and Middle East countries heavily dependent on their oil resources for growth, as well as Brazil, Russia and South Africa, the rich of BRICS countries, (others are India and China). Generally speaking, they are the richest countries among the middle-income group. The "low-income countries" in his categorization are almost all those that have already fallen into the middle-income trap or risk falling into it.

Second, the middle-income trap is a historical concept and might not necessarily match the economic realities of today. Those middle-income countries that had been in trouble before the start of this century were examples of countries that had fallen into the middle-income trap. Although some of them have performed well over the past 10 years, they have not necessarily made the prerequisite shift for them to cross the middle-income trap. We are also not sure that those countries, that have benefited from surging demand as a result of China's strong economic growth and are heavily reliant on exports of their resource products and growth of preliminary industries, will have sufficient growth sustainability to become high-income countries. There are quite a few such examples in history where a country temporarily becomes a high-income economy but, ultimately, is forced back to a lower income level.

Third, the middle-income trap model does not assume absolute convergence, and, therefore, the fact that the growth performance of lower middle-income countries fails to significantly surpass that of upper middle-income countries does not necessarily mean it is illogical. Rather, it is an indication of the middle-income trap. We use the concept of middle-income trap simply to indicate that countries hoping to develop rich economies face the challenge of breaking through the middle-income equilibrium trap, just as those hoping to escape poverty, need to overcome the low-income equilibrium trap.

Implications of China's Economic Growth

In 2010, China became the world's second largest economy and its per capita GDP reached USD 4382, which means that it has just become an upper middle-income country, as categorized by the World Bank. Based on the Maddison standard, or the purchasing power parity method, China has surpassed the USD 7000 point of economic slowdown. If it maintains a 9% annual average growth rate, by 2015, China will reach the higher turning point for economic slowdown, at USD 17,000. Due to many hidden problems and unsustainable factors in its economic growth, Eichengreen *et al.* (2011) warn that there is a 70% possibility of China being subject to the law of economic slowdown. According to some investment economists, however, a 70% possibility of a 2 percentage point decline in the growth rate (which is actually 1.4 percentage points) is not daunting for an economy that has maintained a growth rate of 9–10% over a long period of time.

Population aging is an important cause of the slowing down of economic growth. The growth rate of the working-age population slows and the absolute quantity decreases, and the ratio of the working-age population to the whole population will stop rising before it declines. Accordingly, the economy will no longer benefit as a result of having an ample labor supply and a high savings rate. In 1990, the ratio of people aged 65 years and above to the whole population in Japan was 11.9%. Since then, the dependency ratio, or the ratio of the dependent population to the working-age population, has been rapidly rising. While experiencing such a population structure shift, Japan has seen its economic growth trend suddenly reversed: it first slowed down before stalling (Figure 6.1). In 2010, the ratio of people aged 65 years and above to the whole population in China was 8.9%, which was very close to Japan's level of aging in 1990, when the Japanese economy began to weaken. In the years of the 12th Five-Year Plan period (2011–2015), China, like Japan, will see its dependency ratio rise rapidly.

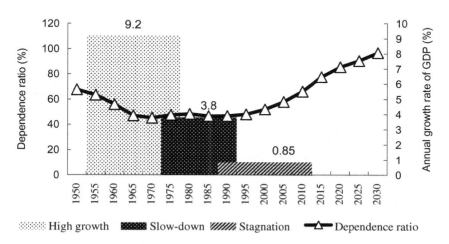

Figure 6.1. Japan's Loss of Population Dividends and Economic Slowdown.

Source: Population data from the UN database; GDP growth rates from the World Bank database and Takeo Hoshi and Anil Kashyap (2011).

In order to prevent abnormal economic slowdown, we should draw lessons from history and work out beneficial solutions. Let us consider Japan again. What we should focus on is not the fact that its growth slowed down from a previous high-rate expansion, but, given the inevitability of the growth slowdown, why it has failed to maintain a growth rate similar to that of Europe and the U.S.

Seen from the perspective of economic growth models, China can also be situated in a special development phase. If we use the analysis framework of Hansen and Prescott (2002) and insert the Lewis dual economy development phase in between the Malthusian growth phase and the Solow growth phase, then it is evident that as the rural surplus labor decreases, labor shortage has become normal and the wage level of ordinary workers has been on the rise. As a result, China's economy has passed the Lewis turning point and has started to shift to the Solow neoclassical growth pattern.

Since 2004, the migrant worker shortage has remained a focus of public attention. Meanwhile, wages of ordinary workers, most noticeably migrant workers, have risen continually from 2004 until today, which is in stark contrast with the previous decades when wage growth virtually stalled. Therefore, if we must choose a year for the Lewis turning point, we would like to use 2004 as the division. Next, we will discuss another important point: the disappearance of population dividends (Cai, 2010). It is predicted that China's dependency ratio will stop falling around 2013 and then start to rise rapidly. This means that China would no longer have the same high levels of saving rate and labor supply to support its dual economic development. Against that backdrop, middle-income countries face unsustainable growth.

On the one hand, rising labor costs will gradually weaken China's comparative advantage and international competitiveness in labor-intensive manufacturing sectors. A corporate survey shows that if labor costs rise by 20%, enterprises in the competitive industries will see their corporate profit margins decline by 20–65% due to the varied labor costs among different industries (Li and Meng, 2011). This will lead to labor-intensive industries moving out of the coastal regions. They might move to neighboring countries with lower labor costs, such as India and Vietnam. They might also move to China's central and western regions. According to the national manufacturing corporate statistics, the share of the labor-intensive manufacturing output of eastern regions to the national total fell from 88.9% in 2004 to 84.7% in 2008, with an average annual decline of more than 1 percentage point.

On the other hand, China still has a long way to go to gain a comparative advantage and international competitiveness in technology-intensive and capital-intensive industries. For example, according to statistics by the China Modernization Strategy Task Force and the China Center for Modernization Research at the Chinese Academy of Sciences (2010, p. 420), China's ratio of R&D to GDP is only 56% and 61% of the level of developed countries and the global average, respectively. The number of R&D staff for every 10,000 population is only 23% and 77%, respectively, of that of the developed world and the global average. The number of patents owned by every 1 million people on average is only 15% and 76% of the level of the developed world and the global average, respectively. In terms of educational level, the average length of education for people aged 30 years in China is only 65% and 67% of the level of the U.S. and Japan, respectively.

Although it has lost its comparative advantage in labor-intensive industries, China has yet to gain a comparative advantage in technology-intensive and capital-intensive sectors, which means the country is facing a "comparative advantage vacuum." Moreover, through its reform and opening-up, China has integrated into the world market. However, it is becoming increasingly challenging for China to further reform and open up to the outside world. These are all typical challenges facing middle-income countries. Therefore, raising the concept of the middle-income trap and a thorough study of related phenomena, as well as the experiences of other economies, are useful for Chinese policy-makers.

Conclusion

The concept of the middle-income trap can be explained within an economic analysis framework and can be verified from economic development experiences. It is also relevant in terms of the sustainability of China's economic growth. Therefore, the concept is useful for academics and policy-makers. Figure 6.2 shows the whole transition process to

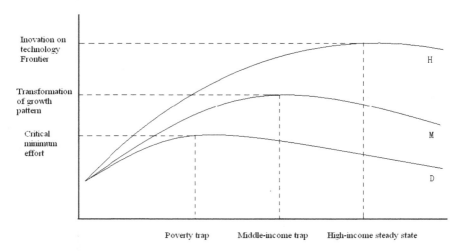

Figure 6.2.   Turning Point of Economic Growth and Breaking-Through Strategy.

high-income economies, from which we can glean the tasks required to
break through the poverty equilibrium trap and the middle-income trap
and make a transition to becoming a high-income economy. We can also
investigate the position of the middle-income trap theory in the development economics framework and its relevant policy implications.

In the process of economic development, an economy initially faces the
vicious cycle of the poverty trap. Its per capita output growth can soon be
offset by population increases and its per capita income can be diluted by
the growth of the population. The standard of living can be maintained at
a subsistence level at best and savings are hard to accumulate. Even if a
technological advancement in the traditional sense occurs, the "critical
minimum effort" of the equilibrium trap cannot be overcome until there is
a revolutionary technological and institutional breakthrough, such as the
application of technologies and market scale expansion resulting from an
industrial revolution, which makes new technologies profitable (Hansen
and Prescott, 2002). Only then can such an equilibrium state be broken.

Unlike the U.S. and European countries, most of the late-comer countries' economies grow within a dual economy framework; the unlimited
labor supply itself favors accumulation of production factors, while population dividends help to improve the savings rate to accelerate capital

formation. Economic restructuring, featuring cross-sector labor movement and migration from rural to urban areas, also leads to reallocation of resources and improvement in total factor productivity. Therefore, in the process of globalization, the dual economy is capable of bringing about a high-rate economic growth. The growth, however, ends with the advent of the Lewis turning point and the loss of population dividends, and the economy might fall into the middle-income trap.

An indispensable prerequisite for breaking the bottleneck brought about by the Lewis turning point and the loss of population dividends and to avoid the middle-income trap is to upgrade the pattern of economic growth from one driven by production factor inputs and resource reallocation effects caused by transition from agriculture to non-agricultural sectors to one driven by improvement in total factor productivity and labor productivity. Once such a shift is made, the long-term economic growth will be built on innovation and it will become sustainable. In this sense, many of the theoretical models and policy suggestions cited in this article are meaningful for helping China cope with the challenges of the middle-income trap.

First, it is urgent to maintain total factor productivity growth. The Solow neoclassical growth model, advocated by Hansen and Prescott, emphasizes that improvement in total factor productivity is the only source to maintain sustainable economic growth. Parente and Prescott (2000) prove that the income gap between different countries is attributable to the differential in their total factor productivity as a result of their respective systems that either encourage or block the adoption of new technologies. Barry Eichengreen and other scholars also find that, typically, the stagnation of total factor productivity can explain 85% of an economy's slowdown. Hayashi and Prescott (2002) show that Japan's economic stagnation is also the result of poor total factor productivity.

Second, it is meaningful to accumulate human resource capital through education and training. Aoki (2011) believes that China has surpassed the Kuznets–Lewis phase and is shifting to the H-phase, centered on human capital accumulation. The success of Japan and Korea in overcoming the middle-income phase is also attributable to their smooth shift from that phase. Human capital is also a source of total factor productivity improvement. Kuijs (2010) shows that in the 1978–2009 period, the annual average growth of total factor productivity was approximately 3.0–3.5%, 0.5 percentage points of which was attributable to improvement in human capital. Whalley and Zhao (2010) also show that human capital plays a role in offsetting the poor performance of total factor productivity.

Finally, deepening system reforms and transforming government functions is a challenging task. Kharas (2011) provides a list of the system reforms that are unavoidable in the transition from a middle-income to high-income phase, such as development of the capital market, acceleration of innovation, development of higher learning, improvement of urban management and city livability, formation of geographical agglomeration, effective rule of law, checks and balances, and the fight against corruption. Moreover, he points out that the real effect of such reforms will take at least years to surface. Japan's economic stagnation after 1990 shows that government function dislocation, especially the failure to establish a mechanism of creative destruction so that the most efficient enterprises can stand out from free competition, ultimately leads to stalling the total factor productivity of the overall economy.

References

Anderson, Jonathan (2011). Chart of the day: Is there really such a thing as a "middle-income trap"? *UBS Investment Research, Emerging Economic Comment*, 21 July.

Aoki, Masahiko (2011). The five-phases of economic development and institutional evolution in China and Japan, Presidential Lecture at the World Congress of International Economic Association Held in Beijing. [Online] Available at: http://papers.ssrn.com/sol3/papers.cfm?abstract_id=1893285. Accessed October 2011.

Ark, Bart van (2008). Performance 2008: Productivity, Employment, and Growth in the World's Economies. *The Conference Board Report*, No. R-1421-08-RR (March).

Athukorala, Prema-Chandra and Wing Thye Woo (2011). Malaysia in the middle-income trap. Paper Prepared for the Asian Economic Panel Meeting at Columbia University, New York City, March 24–25.

Bai, Moo-ki (1982). The Turning Point in the Korean Economy, *Developing Economies*, No. 2, pp. 117–140.

Barro, J. Robert and Xavier Sala-i-Martin (1995). *Economic Growth*. New York: McGraw-Hill, Inc.

Bhagwati, Jagdish N (1996). The miracle that did happen: Understanding East Asia in comparative perspective, Keynote Speech at the Conference on "Government and Market: The Relevance of the Taiwanese Performance to Development Theory and Policy" in honor of Professors Liu and Tsiang, Cornell University, May 3.

Bloom, David and Jeffrey Williamson (1997). Demographic Transitions and Economic Miracles in Emerging Asia, *NBER Working Paper Series*, Working Paper 6268.

Bourgignon, Francois, Fournier, M and Gurgrand, M, (1998). Distribution, development, and education: Taiwan, 1979–1994, Paper presented at LACEA Conference, Buenos Aires.

Cai, Fang (2004). The Consistency of China's Statistics on Employment: Stylized Facts and Implications for Public Policies, *The Chinese Economy*, Vol. 37, No. 5 (September–October), pp. 74–89.

Cai, Fang (2008a). *Lewis Turning Point: A Coming New Stage of China's Economic Development.* China: Social Sciences Academic Press.

Cai, Fang (2008b). Approaching a triumphal span: How far is China towards its Lewisian turning point? *UNU-WIDER Research Paper* No. 2008/09.

Cai, Fang (2009). Future demographic dividend – Tapping the source of China's economic growth, *China Economist*, No. 21 (July–August).

Cai, Fang (2010a). Demographic transition, demographic dividend, and Lewis turning point in China, *China Economic Research Journal*, Vol. 3, No. 4, pp. 4–13.

Cai, Fang (2010b). The formation and evolution of China's migrant labor policy, in *Narratives of Chinese Economic Reforms: How Does China Cross the River?* Zhang, X., Fan, S., and de Haan, A, (eds.), pp. 71–90. World Scientific Publishing Co. Pte. Ltd., New Jersey.

Cai, Fang (2010c). From farmers-turned workers to migrants-turned residents: Urbanization in next decades, Chinese style, *International Economic Review*, No. 2.

Cai, Fang (2010d). The Lewis turning point and the reorientation of public policy, *Social Sciences in China*, Vol. 6, pp. 125–137.

Cai, Fang (2010e). How migrant workers can further contribute to the urbanization: Potentials of China's growth in post-crisis era, *The Chinese Journal of Population Science*, No. 1, pp. 2–10.

Cai, Fang and Dewen Wang (1999). The sustainability of economic growth and the labor contribution, *Economic Research Journal (Jingji Yanjiu)*, No. 10, pp. 62–68.

Cai, Fang and Dewen Wang (2005). China's Demographic Transition: Implications for Growth, *The China Boom and Its Discontents*, in Garnaut and Song (eds.,) Canberra: Asia Pacific Press.

Cai, Fang, Dewen Wang, and Huachu Zhang (2010). Employment Effectiveness of China's Economic Stimulus Package, *China & World Economy*, Vol. 18, No. 1, pp. 33–46.

Cai, Fang and Meiyan Wang (2008). A Counterfactual Analysis on Unlimited Surplus Labor in Rural China, *China & World Economy*, Vol. 16, No. 1, pp. 51–65.

Cai, Fang and Meiyan Wang (2009). The Chinese Employment Situation and Youth Employment Difficulties, *The China Population and Labor Yearbook Volume 10: The Sustainability of Economic Growth from the Perspective of Human Resources*in Cai, Fang (ed.,), Beijing: Social Sciences Academic Press (China).

Cai, Fang and Meiyan Wang (2010). Growth and Structural Changes in Employment in Transition China, *Journal of Comparative Economics*, Vol. 38, pp. 71–81.

Cai, Fang, Meiyan Wang, and Yue Qu (2009). Industrial and Labor Relocations among Chinese Regions, *The Chinese Industrial Economics*, No. 8, pp. 5–16.

Cai Fang and Meng Xin (2004). *Population change, System Transition and Sustained Retirement Security Pattern*. Edition 10 of "*Comparative Studies*".

Cai, Fang, Yang Du and Changbao Zhao (2007). Regional Labour Market Integration since China's World Trade Organization Entry: Evidence from Household-level Data, *China – Linking Markets for Growth*, in Garnaut, Ross and Ligang Song (eds), Canberra: Asia Pacific Press, pp. 133–150.

Cai, F., Du, Y., and Wang, M. (2001). Household Registration System and Labor Market Protection, *Economic Research Journal (Jingji Yanjiu)*, No. 12, pp. 41–49.

Cai, Fang, Yang Du, and Wenshu Gao (2004). Employment Elasticity, Natural Unemployment, and Macroeconomic Policies, *Journal of Economic Research*, No. 9, pp. 18–25, 47.

Cai Fang and Zhang Chewei etc. (2002). *What Population Will Bring for China?* Guangdong Education Press in Guangzhou.

Chan, K.W. (2010). The Household Registration System and Migrant Labor in China: Notes on a Debate, *Population and Development Review*, Vol. 36, No. 2, pp. 357–364.

Chan, K.W. and Buckingham, W. (2008). Is China Abolishing the Hukou System? *The China Quarterly*, Vol. 195, pp. 582–606.

Chang, H. (2010). Agriculture, Countryside, and Farmers: Challenges Facing the Next Five-year Plan, *Century Weekly*, No. 34, pp. 40–41.

Caldwell, John C (1976). Toward a Restatement of Demographic Transition Theory, *Population and Development Review*, Vol. 2, pp. 321–366.

Capital University of Economics and Business Task Group (2007). *Studies on Chinese Populations' Death and Life Expectancy*, published in "*Research Report on National Population Development Strategy*" of the National

Population Development Strategy Research Task Group, Chinese Population Press in Beijing.

Carter, Colin, Zhong Funing, and Cai Fang (1996). *China's Ongoing Reform of Agriculture*. San Francisco: 1990 Institute.

China Development Research Foundation (2005). *Human Development Report 2005 — Seeking Fair Human Development*, China Translation & Publishing Corporation in Beijing.

China Modernization Strategy Task Force and China Center for Modernization Research of the Chinese Academy of Social Sciences (2010). *China Modernization Report 2010 — Summary of World Modernization*. Beijing: Peking University Press (in Chinese).

Chun, Natalie (2010). Middle Class Size in the Past, Present, and Future: A Description of Trends in Asia, *ADB Working Paper Series*, No. 217, September.

Department of Rural Survey of National Bureau of Statistics (DRS-NBS) (2010). A Mornitoring Survey Report on Migrant Workers in 2009, *Report on China's Population and Labor (No. 11): Labor Market Challenges in the Post-crisis Era*, in Cai, Fang (ed.), Beijing: Social Sciences Academic Press (China).

Department of Survey and Statistics, People's Bank of China (DSS-PBC) (2010). The 5th Monitoring Report on Migrant Workers, *Report on China's Population and Labor (No. 11): Labor Market Challenges in the Post-crisis Era*, in Cai, Fang (ed.), Beijing: Social Sciences Academic Press (China).

Department of Rural Social and Economic Survey, National Bureau of Statistics (NBS-DORSES) (various years). *China Yearbook of Rural Household Survey*. Beijing: China Statistics Press.

Du, Yang (2004). The Formation of Low Fertility and Its Impacts on Long term Economic Growth in China, *The World Economy*, No. 12, pp. 14–23.

Du, Yang and Meiyan Wang (2010). New Estimate of Surplus Rural Labor Force and Its Implications, *Journal of Guangzhou University* (Social Science Edition), Vol. 9, No. 4, pp. 17–24.

Eeckhout, Jan and Boyan Jovanovic, (2007). Occupational choice and development, *NBER Working Paper Series*, No. 13686, National Bureau of Economic Research, Massachusetts.

Eichengreen, Barry, Donghyun Park, and Kwanho Shin, (2011). When fast growing economies slow down: International evidence and implications for China, *NBER Working Paper*, No. 16919, National Bureau of Economic Research, Massachusetts.

Fields, Gary S. (1998). Accounting for Income Inequality and its Change, Mimeo, Cornell University

Fogel, Robert W. (2007). Capitalism and Democracy in 2040: Forecasts and Speculations, *NBER Working Paper*, No. 13184.

Freeman, Richard (1993). Labor Market and Institutions in Economic Development, *AEA Papers and Proceedings*, pp. 403–408.

Garrett, Geoffrey, (2004). Globalization's Missing Middle, *Foreign Affaires,* Vol. 83, No. 6, pp. 84–96.

Hansen, D. Gary and Edward C. Prescott, (2002). Malthus to Solow, *American Economic Review*, Vol. 92, No. 4, pp. 1205–1217.

Hayashi, Fumio and Edward C. Prescott (2002). The 1990s in Japan: A Lost Decade, *Review of Economic Dynamics*, Vol. 5, (1), pp. 206–235.

Hayami, Yūjirō and Yoshihisa Gōdo, (2009). *Development Economics: From the Poverty to the Wealth of Nations*. Beijing: China Social Sciences Academic Press.

Herrmann-Pillath, Carsten and Xingyuan Feng (2004). Competitive Governments, Fiscal Arrangements, and the Provision of Local Public Infrastructure in China: A Theory-driven Study of Gujiao Municipality, *China Information*, Vol. 18, No. 3, pp. 373–428.

Hirschman, Albert O. (1970). *Exit, Voice, and Loyalty: Responses to Decline in Firms, Organizations, and State*. Cambridge, MA: Harvard University Press.

Hu, Ying (2009). Predictions on Working Age Population of Rural and Urban China. Unpublished memo.

Indermit, Gill and Homi Kharas, (2008). *An East Asian Renaissance: Ideas for Economic Growth*. Beijing: CITIC Press Corporation (in Chinese).

Japan Center for Economic Research (JCER) (2007). *Demographic Change and the Asian Economy*. Tokyo: Long-term Forecast Team of Economic Research Department, Japan Center for Economic Research.

Jin, H., Qian, Y., and Weingast, B.R. (2005). Regional Decentralization and Fiscal Incentives: Federalism, Chinese Style, *Journal of Public Economics*, Vol. 89, pp. 1719–1742.

Knight, John and Lina Song (2005). *Towards a Labour Market in China*. New York: Oxford University Press.

Kojima, Kiyoshi (2000). The "Flying Geese" Model of Asian Economic Development: Origin, Theoretical Extensions, and Regional Policy Implications, *Journal of Asian Economics*, Vol. 11, pp. 375–401.

Kharas, Homi, (2011). China's shift to a high-income country-method to avoid middle-income trap, *Long-Term Development and Transition of the Chinese Economy*, in Chonggeng Lin and Andrew Michael Spence, (eds), CITIC Publishing House, pp. 470–501.

Krugman, Paul (1994). The Myth of Asia's Miracle, *Foreign Affairs* (November/ December).

Kuijs, Louis, (2010). China through 2020 — A macroeconomic scenario, *World Bank China Research Working Paper* No. 9, World Bank, Washington, D.C.

Lau, Laurence J. (2010a). Expansion of Domestic Demand is Fourfold, *China News Website*. Available at: http://www.chinanews.com.cn/cj/cj-ylgd/news/2010/01-18/2077952.shtml. Accessed on Jan 21 2013.

Lau, Lawrence J. (2010b). The Chinese Economy: The Next Thirty Years, presented at The Institute of Quantitative and Technical Economics, Chinese Academy of Social Sciences, Beijing, 16 January.

Li, Huiyong and Xiangjuan Meng (2010). Rising labor cost will change corporate profit landscape-a comparative study of labor cost, inflation and corporate profit, *SWS Research*, 1 July.

Lee, Ronald and Andrew Mason (2006). What Is the Demographic Dividend? *Finance and Development*, Vol. 43, No. 3, pp. 16–17.

Lewis, W. A. (1954). Economic Development with Unlimited Supplies of Labour, *The Manchester School of Economic and Social Studies,* 22, Vol. pp. 139–191, Reprinted in A. N. Agarwala and S. P. Singh (eds.), *The Economics of Underdevelopment.* Bombay: Oxford University Press, 1958.

Lewis, Arthur (1958). Unlimited Labour: Further Notes, The Manchester School, Vol. 26 (Jan), pp. 1–32.

Lewis, Arthur (1972). Reflections on Unlimited Labour, *International Economics and Development*, in Di Marco, L. (ed.), New York: Academic Press, pp. 75–96.

Li, L. (2009). Why Has the Share of University Students of Rural Origins Been Halved? *Guangzhou Daily*, Jan 24.

Lin, Justin Yifu (2006). Development Strategy, Population and Population Policies, *China's Population and Economic Development in 21st Century*, in Yi, Zeng, Ling Li, Baochang Gu, and Yifu Lin (eds.), China: Social Sciences Academic Press.

Minami, Ryoshin and Xinxin Ma (2009). The Turning Point of Chinese Economy: Compared with Japanese Experience, *Asian Economics*, Vol. 50, No. 12, pp. 2–20 (in Japanese).

Minami, Ryoshin (1968). The Turning Point in the Japanese Economy, *The Quarterly Journal of Economics*, Vol. 82, No. 3, pp. 380–402.

Minami, Ryoshin (1998). Economic Development and Income Distribution in Japan: An Assessment of the Kuznets Hypothesis, *Cambridge Journal of Economics*, Vol. 22, No. 1, pp. 39–58.

Minami, Ryoshin (2010). Turning Point in the Japanese Economy, presented at the Workshop in the Project of Institute of Asian Cultures Toyo University "The Discussion on the Changes in East Asia Labor Market Based on Lewisian Turning Point Theory", Tokyo, 18th–19th, July 2010.

Minami, Ryoshin and Akira Ono (1981). Behavior of Income Shares in a Labor Surplus Economy: Japan's Experience, *Economic Development and Cultural Change*, Vol. 29, No. 2, pp. 309–324.

Minami, Ryoshin and Xinxin Ma (2010). The Turning Point of Chinese Economy: Comparison with Japanese Experience, *China Economic Journal*, Vol. 3, No. 2, pp. 163–179.

Minami, Ryoshin (1968). The Turning Point in the Japanese Economy, *The Quarterly Journal of Economics*, Vol. 82, No. 3, pp. 380–402.

Morduch, Jonathan and Terry Sicular (2002). Rethinking Inequality Decomposition, with Evidence from Rural China, *Economic Journal*, Vol. 112, No. 476, pp. 93–106.

Moriguchi, Chiaki and Emmanuel Saez (2008). *The Review of Economics and Statistics*, Vol. 90, No. 4, pp. 713–734.

National Bureau of Statistics (2009). *China Statistical Yearbook, 2009*. China Statistical Publishing House, Beijing.

National Development and Restructuring Commission (NDRC) (2010). *Report on Implementation of 2009 Plan of National Economic and Social Developments and on Draft of 2010 Plan of National Economic and Social Developments*, presented at 3rd Session of 11th National People's Congress of China.

Notestein, Frank W. (1945). Population — The Long View, *Food for the World*, in Theodore W. Schultz (ed.), Chicago: University of Chicago Press.

Oi, J. C. (1999). Local State Corporatism, *Rural China Takes Off: Institutional Foundations of Economic Reform*, in J. Oi (ed.), Berkeley: University of California Press.

Olson, M. (1985). The Exploitation and Subsidization of Agriculture in the Developing and Developed Countries, Paper presented to the 19th Conference of International Association of Agricultural Economists, Malaga, Spain.

Parente, Stephen L. and Edward C. Prescott (2000). *Barriers to Riches*. Cambridge, MA: The MIT Press.

Qu Yue (2009). Demographic dividend: Continuation or Substitution, *Green Book of Chinese Population and Labor No. 9*, Cai, Fang (ed.), Social Sciences Academic Press in Beijing.

Ranis, Gustav (2004). Arthur Lewis' Contribution to Development Thinking and Policy, Yale University Economic Growth Center Discussion Paper No. 891 (August).

Ranis, Gustav and Fei, John C. H. (1961). A Theory of Economic Development, *The American Economic Review*, Vol. 51, No. 4, pp. 533–565.

Ravallion, Martin and Shaohua Chen (1999). When Economic Reform Is Faster Than Statistical Reform: Measuring and Explaining Income Inequality in Rural China, *Oxford Bulletin of Economics and Statistics*, Vol. 61, No. 1, pp. 33–56.

Rawski, Thomas G. (2001). What's Happening to China's GDP Statistics? *China Economic Review,* Vol. 12, No. 4, pp. 298–302.

Roberts, Kenneth, Rachel Connelly, Zhenming Xie, and Zhenzhen Zheng (2004). Patterns of Temporary Labor Migration of Rural Women from Anhui and Sichuan, *The China Journal*, No. 52, pp. 49–70.

Ru, Xin, Xueyi Lu, and Peilin Li (2008). *Analysis and Prospects on China's Social Situation, 2009*. China: Social Sciences Academic Press.

Sala-i-Martin, X. X. (1996). The Classical Approach to Convergence Analysis, *The Economic Journal*, Vol. 106 (July), pp. 1019–1036.

Sala-i-Martin, X. X. (1997). I Just Ran Two Million Regressions, *Papers and Proceedings of the Hundred and Fourth Annual Meeting of the American Economic Association, American Economic Review*, Vol. 87, No. 2, pp. 178–183.

Sheng, Laiyun (2009). New Challenges Migrants Are Faced with on Employment during the Financial Crisis, paper for the conference "Urban-rural Social Welfare Integration", Chengdu, Sichuan Province, April 16.

Solinger, Dorothy J. (2001). Why We Cannot Count the Unemployed? *The China Quarterly*, No. 167 (August), pp. 671–688.

Solow, Robert M. (1956). A Contribution to the Theory of Economic Growth, *Quarterly Journal of Economics*, Vol. 70, No. 1, pp. 65–94.

Spence, Michael, Edwin Lim, Paul Romer, and Ian Porter (2010). Building the Foundation of a High Income Economy: Suggestions for China's 12th Five Year Plan from an International Perspective.

Taylor, J.R. (1993). Rural Employment Trends and the Legacy of Surplus Labor, 1978–1989, in *Economic Trends in Chinese Agriculture: The Impact of Post-Mao Reforms*, Y. Y. Kueh and R. F. Ash (eds.), Oxford University Press, New York.

Takeo, Hoshi and Anil Kashyap (2011). Why did Japan stop growing? *National Institute for Research Advancement (NIRA) Working Paper,* October. [online]. Available from: http://www.nira.or.jp/pdf/1002english_report.pdf, 2011.

Theodore, Schultz (1999). *Transforming Traditional Agriculture*. Beijing: the Commercial Press (in Chinese).

Tiebout, C. (1956). A Pure Theory of Local Expenditures, *The Journal of Political Economy*, Vol. 64, No. 5, pp. 416–424.

The World Bank (1997). *China 2020: Development Challenges in the New Century*. World Bank, Washington, D.C.

The World Bank (2010). *China: A Vision for Pension Policy Reform, Vol. I: Main Report*. Human Development Unit, East Asia and Pacific Region, April 30.

Turner, Adair (2006). Pension Challenges in an Aging World, *Finance and Development*, Vol. 43, No. 3, pp. 36–39.

United Nations (2003). *World Population Prospects: the 2002 Revision*. United Nations Population Division, Department of Economic and Social Affairs / United Nations Population Division.

United Nations (2009). *The World Population Prospects: The 2008 Revision*. Available at: http://esa.un.org/unpp/. Accessed on Dec. 20, 2009.

Walder, Andrew (1995). Local Governments As Industrial Firms, *American Journal of Sociology*, 101(2).

Wang, Dewen and Fang Cai (2009). The Education and Employment of Rural and Urban Youth in China, *The China Population and Labor Yearbook Volume 10: The Sustainability of Economic Growth from the Perspective of Human Resources*, in Cai, Fang (ed.), Beijing: Social Sciences Academic Press (China).

Wang, Meiyan (2007). Changes of Discrimination against Migrant Workers in China's Urban Labor Market, *China Labor Economics*, Vol. 4, No. 1, pp. 109–119.

Wang, Meiyan (2009). Educational Return and Educational Resource Allocation between Rural and Urban Areas — An Empirical Analysis Using China's Urban Labor Survey Data, *World Economy*, No. 5, pp. 3–17.

Wang, Meiyan (2009). Universal High School and Mass Higher Education, *The China Population and Labor Yearbook Volume 10: The Sustainability of Economic Growth from the Perspective of Human Resources*, in Cai, Fang (ed.), Beijing: Social Sciences Academic Press (China).

Wang, Meiyan (2010). The Rise of Labor Cost and the Fall of Labor Input: Has China Reached Lewis Turning Point? *China Economic Journal*, Vol. 3, No. 2, pp. 139–155.

Wang, Meiyan and Fang Cai (2008). Gender Earnings Differential in Urban China, *Review of Development Economics*, Vol. 12, No. 2, pp. 442–454.

Wang Guangzhou and Niu Jianlin (2009). Forecast on Present Situation, Issues and Development of Chinese Education Quantum Structure, *Green Book of Chinese Population and Labor No. 9*, Cai Fang (ed.), Social Sciences Academic Press in Beijing.

Walder, A. (1995). Local Governments As Industrial Firms, *American Journal of Sociology*, Vol. 101, No. 2, pp. 47–70.

Wang, Meiyan and Cai, F. (2010). Future Prospects of Household Registration System Reform, in *The China Population and Labor Yearbook Volume 2: The Sustainability of Economic Growth from the Perspective of Human Resources*, F. Cai, Brill, Boston (eds.).

Wang, Qing, Stephen Zhang, and Ernest Ho (2009). Chinese economy through 2020: It's not whether but how growth will decelerate, *Morgan Stanley China Economy*, Morgan Stanley Research Asia/Pacific, 20 September.

Weller, Christian (2000). Raising the Retirement Age: The Wrong Direction for Social Security, *Economic Policy Institute Briefing Paper* (September).

Whalley, John and Xiliang Zhao (2010). The contribution of human capital to China's economic growth, *NBER Working Paper* No. 16592, National Bureau of Economic Research, Massachusetts.

Whyte, M.K. (2010). The Paradoxes of Rural-Urban Inequality in Contemporary China, in *One Country, Two Societies: Rural-Urban Inequality in Contemporary China*, M.K. White (ed.), Harvard University Press, Cambridge.

Yao, Yang and Ke Zhang (2010). Has China Passed the Lewis Turning Point? A Structural Estimation Based on Provincial Data, *China Economic Journal*, Vol. 3, No. 2, pp. 155–162.

Young, Alwyn (1992). A Tale of Two Cities: Factor Accumulation and Technical Change in Hong Kong and Singapore, *NBER Macroeconomics Annual*, in Olivier Blanchard and Stanley Fischer (eds.), Cambridge, Mass.: MIT Press.

Young, Alwyn (1994). The Tyranny of Numbers: Confronting the Statistical Realities of the East Asian Growth Experience, *NBER Working Paper*, No. 4680 (March).

Yu, Xuejun (2002). Estimation on Magnitude and Structure of 5th National Population Census, *Population Research*, Vol. 26, No. 3, pp. 9–15.

Zhang, Junsen, Yaohui Zhao, Albert Park, and Xiaoqing Song (2005). Economic Returns to Schooling in Urban China, 1988 to 2001, *Journal of Comparative Economics*, Vol. 33, pp. 730–752.

Zhang, Xiaojian (ed.) (2008) *The Reforms and Developments of the Chinese Employment*. Beijing: China Labor and Social Security Press.

Zhang, Xiaobo, Jin Yang, and Shenglin Wang (2010). China Has Reached the Lewis Turning Point, *Journal of Zhejiang University (Edition of Humanities and Social Sciences)*, Vol. 40, No. 1, pp. 54–72.

Index